The Sacred Art of
Forgiveness

Forgiving Ourselves and Others through God's Grace

Marcia Ford

Walking Together, Finding the Way®
SKYLIGHT PATHS®
PUBLISHING
Woodstock, Vermont

The Sacred Art of Forgiveness:
Forgiving Ourselves and Others through God's Grace

2011 Quality Paperback Edition, Second Printing

Library of Congress Cataloging-in-Publication Data
Ford, Marcia.
The sacred art of forgiveness : forgiving ourselves and others through God's grace / by Marcia Ford.
p. cm.
Includes bibliographical references.
ISBN-13: 978-1-59473-175-4
ISBN-10: 1-59473-175-6
1. Forgiveness—Religious aspects. 2. Reconciliation—Religious aspects. I. Title.

BL65.F67F67 2006
204—dc22

2006001885

10 9 8 7 6 5 4 3 2

Manufactured in the United States of America
Cover Design: Sara Dismukes

SkyLight Paths Publishing is creating a place where people of different spiritual traditions come together for challenge and inspiration, a place where we can help each other understand the mystery that lies at the heart of our existence.

SkyLight Paths sees both believers and seekers as a community that increasingly transcends traditional boundaries of religion and denomination—people wanting to learn from each other, *walking together, finding the way.*

SkyLight Paths, "Walking Together, Finding the Way," and colophon are trademarks of LongHill Partners, Inc., registered in the U.S. Patent and Trademark Office.

Walking Together, Finding the Way®
Published by SkyLight Paths Publishing
A Division of LongHill Partners, Inc.
Sunset Farm Offices, Route 4, P.O. Box 237
Woodstock, VT 05091
Tel: (802) 457-4000   Fax: (802) 457-4004
www.skylightpaths.com

As always, to a family that has survived
the fallout from my deadline-driven vocation.
John, Elizabeth, and Sarah, you have forgiven much more,
and much more often, than I deserve.

Contents

Contents

Introduction

I was nearly twenty years old before I understood what it meant to truly forgive someone. At the time, I felt ancient, much too old to be learning such a basic life lesson. How come no one had ever explained this amazing, life-transforming concept to me before?

Now, some thirty-five years later, I realize how young I was to be learning such an incredible skill—an art, and a sacred one at that. I've had to relearn and refine that art over the years, of course, and at times, my willingness and ability to forgive has been tested to the max. But between my own experiences and my observation of others' experiences, I have become convinced that learning to forgive is one of life's greatest lessons.

For me, that first lesson in radical forgiveness came at a price that many people would understandably be unwilling to pay. As a college freshman in the late 1960s, I had already been immersed in a hedonistic, "If-it-feels-good-do-it" lifestyle for several years. Problem was, what felt good at the moment felt pretty crummy later on, but I had no idea how to stop doing what felt good. My friends were as little help to me as I was to them; we would not admit to each other that an abundance of free love and a perpetual state of altered consciousness didn't necessarily result in good mental health. By the spring of my freshman year, I could best be described as a wreck. I needed professional help, but the only thing I could think to do was seek out the personal advice of someone older and supposedly wiser.

So I paid a visit to this older and wiser someone, a man I had known all my life and would have trusted with that life. If anyone had my back, it was Elmer. (No, that's not his real name. I've found that it sometimes helps to think of your offender as a cartoon character, and Elmer Fudd works just fine in this case.) Elmer had always been there for me, and Elmer would be there to help me find my way out of the psychedelic maze I was living in.

You know what's coming, right? Sure enough, before I could tell Mr. Fudd why I was at his door, he began to come on to me. I won't go into the gories. Let's just say his intentions were obvious. I managed to extricate myself from the situation, and I returned home physically unmolested but emotionally shattered. What Elmer managed to do was set me up for even more wreckage. As a result, I have only fragmented memories of one entire year of college, and I can't exactly vouch for any of the other years either.

Neither my behavior nor my memory loss is entirely Elmer's fault, of course, and I've never blamed my subsequent downward spiral on him. There's so much I can blame him for that there's no need to overdo it. He obviously betrayed my trust in him and sought to take advantage of me at a highly vulnerable time in my life. He cheapened our lifelong relationship and treated me in a way that no woman should ever be treated. His behavior was repulsive and lecherous and frightening. But this was not some raincoat flasher on the seedy side of Manhattan, someone I could dismiss as a creepy sicko. This was someone I would have to have contact with in the future.

On my way toward a lifetime of bitterness, resentment, and exceedingly awkward social engagements, I came upon a bend in the road—a personal encounter with none other than God. No one was more surprised than I that the God I had so assiduously avoided turned out to be personally interested in me and relentlessly forgiving of the disinterest I had historically shown in return. This was very cool indeed, but again— there was that price tag. God, as it turned out, seemed to expect me to be relentlessly forgiving as well.

I believe with every fiber of my being that God would love me even if I wasn't the forgiving sort. But early on, I realized that God really did know what was best for me and that by cooperating with the Spirit of God I'd do a whole lot better in life than I would if left to my own devices. Given that my own devices had routinely malfunctioned up to that point, cooperation was a no-brainer.

I'm not saying that judgmentalism was one of my primary character flaws or anything, but for whatever reason it became clear that Job One on God's to-do list for me was "Learn to see other people as God sees them." That was all well and good, except for the fact that "other people" included Elmer, who was not a cartoon character but a flesh-and-blood child of God. And I would have to forgive him.

Since that time, I've learned a great deal about forgiveness, and not just because I've had to ask for it so often. Having experienced its power in my own life, I became something of an amateur observer of how forgiveness works in a person's life, what it looks like, and what kind of an impact it has on the forgiver and the forgiven alike.

I've also observed what its absence looks like, and I can assure you, that doesn't make for a pretty picture. Early on I realized that unforgiveness equals ugliness, and that revelation clearly tipped the scales in favor of developing a forgiving spirit.

Couple my observation of the act of forgiveness with my occupation as a journalist and author, and what you end up with is a book. This one. But why? Why do we need another book on forgiveness? I have the answer to that one: because we do. Because forgiveness is in such short supply, we need to keep preaching the message, hearing the message, and living the message.

And then there's the matter of the different and distinct ways in which we each grab hold of a spiritual reality. For some people, a step-by-step how-to book on forgiveness is just what they need. Others may be better able to grasp the concept through an academic book. You can have ten books on forgiveness by ten different authors, and each one will appeal to a different sort of reader.

If you gravitate toward more reflective and highly personal types of books, then you're my kind of reader. You'll get what I'm saying right away, which means this book stands a good chance of changing your life for the better.

If that should happen to you, promise you'll let me know? I'd love to hear from you.

One important note: Throughout, I've used the male pronoun when referring to God. I'm fully aware of the feminine characteristics of God, just as I am aware of the conflicts that arise when gender-specific pronouns are used. But at heart I am a writer, and I believe in communicating clearly rather than muddying up the text to satisfy a variety of theological tastes. Where possible, I avoid the use of pronouns. But it isn't always possible, at least not without ending up with a host of annoying sentences. Forgive me, okay?

Why Bother?

Before we begin to discover what forgiveness is and what it isn't, we need to look at an even more fundamental issue: the question of *why* it's important to forgive. I'll go back yet another step and tell you why it's important to start with that question: because that's where most people generally start.

Try it for yourself. Suggest that your friend forgive her significant other for sending an innocuous reply to an e-mail from an old girlfriend, and listen for the first thing out of her mouth. I can guarantee that it won't be a definition of forgiveness. It will likely be a mix of indignant exclamations and equally indignant questions: "*Forgive* him? Why should I *forgive* him? I'll never do that! Forgive him? No way!"

No, she won't start with a definition.

We're so sure that we know what forgiveness is that we skip the defining step entirely. We go straight to the part where we push our nose out of joint, stiffen our back, and express our righteous anger while alternately huffing and puffing.

It is impossible even to begin the act of loving one's enemies without the prior acceptance of the necessity, over and over again, of forgiving those who inflict evil and injury upon us.

—MARTIN LUTHER KING JR.

Forgiveness is a gift of high value. Yet its cost is nothing.

—BETTY SMITH

And the questions just keep coming.

Why bother? Why should I forgive someone who has hurt me? Why should he have the satisfaction of knowing I have forgiven him, after he betrayed me? If I forgive him, won't he see that as a license to keep on hurting me, expecting me to forgive him again and again? It's just not fair.

Well, no, it's not fair. Forgiveness isn't about fairness. Neither is it about asking for more trouble from the one who did you wrong. In fact, it's not even about the offender.

Forgiveness is mostly about you.

That's right. It's about you letting go of your past, changing your present, and protecting your future. It's about making a better life for yourself, and in some small way, making a better world as well.

It's about the best part of you, those noble character traits that come together in one magnificent, grand gesture that proves your mettle—courage, humility, compassion, fortitude, resilience, grace. It's about the gifts of the Spirit you exhibit and the gifts you receive—love, joy, peace, patience, kindness, goodness, faith, gentleness, and self-control—each time you extend forgiveness to another person.

And still, the questions won't go away. Questions like these:

- Isn't forgiveness a sign of weakness?
- What if the person doesn't show any remorse?
- Will I have to let my sister back into my life after I've forgiven her?

- I thought I'd forgiven my ex-husband, but I can't forget what he did to me. Do I have to forget in order to truly forgive?

- What's in it for me? I mean, I'm the one who's been brutalized; I'm the one who needs healing. What do I have to gain by forgiving that monster?

- How can I be sure she won't hurt me again?

- I don't need to forgive anyone; I'm the one who needs to be forgiven. How can I get over the shame I feel and not be so afraid to ask for forgiveness?

- I keep going over the crummy situation I'm in, looking for someone to blame. But the only one I can blame is God. Is it possible for me to forgive *God*?

- The Bible says I have to forgive the same person a crazy number of times. Is that true?

Those are all valid questions about forgiveness, which is nearly always possible to grant, and reconciliation, which is not always possible or even desirable. What's disturbing about some of the questions, though, is the number of underlying misconceptions about forgiveness that they reveal. Until those misconceptions are corrected, we may have a hard time understanding why we should bother forgiving our offenders.

> Never forget the three powerful resources you always have available to you: love, prayer, and forgiveness.
>
> —H. JACKSON BROWN, JR.

3

Once we have a better grasp on forgiveness, we may have a hard time understanding why we didn't bother sooner.

REFLECTION

Reflect on this thought, from the web log of Baptist pastor Gordon Atkinson on the website www.reallivepreacher.com:

> It really doesn't matter if the person who hurt you deserves to be forgiven. Forgiveness is a gift you give yourself. You have things to do, and you want to move on.

Think about each sentence and how it applies to your life. How do you feel about forgiving a person who doesn't deserve it? Do you consider forgiveness to be a gift to yourself? Do you believe that forgiving someone who has offended you can help you get on with your life?

PRACTICE

Write your own list of questions about forgiveness. What, if anything, would you like to understand better about the concept of forgiveness? The concept of reconciliation? In your previous experiences with both concepts, think about what went right and what went wrong, and express your impressions in the form of questions that you hope to have answered.

He who has not forgiven an enemy has not yet tasted one of the most sublime enjoyments of life.

—JOHANN K. LAVATER

For example, let's say you recently reconciled with your girl-friend, but now you're having second thoughts. You might express your misgivings in this way: Should I have given this more time? Did we reconcile too soon? Does she really understand how much she hurt me? Why do I still have this feeling that I can't trust her?

Even if you haven't found the answers to your own questions by the end of this book, you will have clarified your thoughts on the situation, and you'll be able to seek out the answers on your own.

Humanity is never so beautiful as when praying for forgiveness, or else forgiving another.

—JEAN PAUL RICHTER

2

An Act of Love

When I discovered I was pregnant with my first child, I read every article and book I could get my hands on about pregnancy, childbirth, and child-rearing. And of course, every woman in my life who ever had a child offered advice on everything from the best foods to eat while breastfeeding to preparing for my child's first day of school.

But no one prepared me for the astonishing realization that I had known little about love before the day my daughter was born. I thought I was well acquainted with love in all its spiritual, physical, and emotional glory, but on that day I discovered this new and deeper lesson about love: love is knowing you'd take a bullet to save your child's life.

That's a far cry from the kind of love that accompanies many of our acts of forgiveness. And there are many levels of love that lie between the love of a parent for a child and the love that God gives us, say, to be able to forgive a stranger who ran a red light and killed a woman and her unborn twins. The latter is nothing like the various kinds of love we associate with family, friends, or romantic partners. Some kinds of love come to us naturally; others can come no other way but supernaturally.

Forgiving a person who has hurt us deeply is contrary to human nature, which is exactly why we need to draw on super-human power to accomplish it. But then God pulls a fast one on us; the power to forgive goes hand-in-hand with the power to love. Lo and behold, there we are, dumbstruck by the love we have for someone we had only planned to forgive.

We can reject that love, I suppose, but then the forgiveness wouldn't be genuine forgiveness. "The choice to follow love through to its completion is the choice to seek completion within ourselves," bestselling author Marianne Williamson writes in her book *Illuminata*. "Forgiveness does not mean that we suppress anger; forgiveness means that we have asked for a miracle: the ability to see through mistakes that someone has made to the truth that lies in all of our hearts." We do indeed ask for a miracle each time we grant forgiveness—a miracle of supernatural love for someone we may have once considered to be an enemy.

Martin Luther King Jr. knew what it meant to forgive his enemies and experience a profound love for them despite the injustices they inflicted on others. One of the reasons his repu-tation has steadily grown over the years is that people have become increasingly aware of the deep and abiding love he had for everyone. Once the dust of the civil rights movement set-tled, we could see more clearly the dichotomy between the hateful anger of militants and the righteous anger of King.

Forgiveness is love practiced among peo-ple who love poorly. It sets us free without wanting anything in return.

—HENRI NOUWEN

Resentment toward any human being can-not exist in the same heart with love to God.

—WILLIAM T. HAM

King so successfully lived out so many of the truths in the Scriptures that he left us without excuse for failing to do the same. Jesus says to "love your enemies and pray for those who persecute you" (Matt. 5:44); between the impossibility of being like Jesus and the familiarity of those words, we find it easy to weasel our way out of following them. And then along comes a man like King, loving his enemies and praying for those who openly persecuted him and making us look bad. It *is* possible, he says through his actions; it *is* possible to "Be angry and yet ... not sin" (Eph. 4:26), to "Bless those who persecute you; bless and do not curse" (Rom. 12:14), to "Love your enemies, do good to those who hate you" (Luke 6:27, NAS).

"Love is the only force capable of transforming an enemy into a friend," King once said. "We never get rid of an enemy by meeting hate with hate; we get rid of an enemy by getting rid of enmity. By its very nature, hate destroys and tears down; by its very nature, love creates and builds up. Love transforms with redemptive power."[1] Love may not transform your enemy into a friend, but the point is that it could; it has that kind of power.

If you've forgiven someone but can't bring yourself to say you love him, no need to be concerned. Forgiveness is so closely linked with love that it's nearly impossible to have one without the other; there's a good chance that you're confusing the gift of supernatural love with the feeling of love. One is a spiritual reality, the other a human emotion.

Today I forgive all those who have ever offended me. I give my love to all thirsty hearts, both to those who love me and to those who do not love me.

—PARAMAHANSA
YOGANANDA

8

REFLECTION

What are the lessons love has taught you? Are you able to make a distinction between love as a supernatural gift and love as a natural human feeling? Many people believe love is a choice we make each day. How has that played out in your life?

PRACTICE

Ask God to infuse you with a supernatural love for someone you've had a hard time liking. It doesn't have to be an enemy, just someone who grates on you. Pray that the Spirit will love the person through you, and ask how you can perform loving acts for that person until your love for him kicks in. Then go out and do what you feel the Spirit is leading you to do.

The man who foolishly does me wrong, I will return to him the protection of my most ungrudging love; and the more evil comes from him, the more good shall go from me.

—BUDDHA

3 It Starts with You

Barbara has been estranged from her brother for so long that she eventually lost track of him entirely. That would have been okay with her five years ago; back then, she didn't much care whether she ever saw him again or not. He had lived with Barbara and her husband for a few months after being released from rehab, but she had kicked him out after she smelled beer on his breath. Or what she thought was beer. She began to wonder if she had been wrong.

Some time later, Barbara and her husband began to realize that little things were missing—mostly small but valuable items like seldom-used jewelry and a few collectible coins. In anger, she called her brother and accused him of stealing from her; yes, he admitted, he had taken a few things and sold them so he could find a place to live. Furious, Barbara hung up and swore she would have nothing to do with him until he apologized and asked her forgiveness.

Within three years, both of Barbara's parents died, and she felt a compelling need to be reconciled with her brother, the only surviving member of her biological family. Today she lives with the regret that she never forgave him, sought his forgiveness, or attempted to reconcile with him when she had the chance. She prays regularly that he'll somehow reappear on someone's radar screen so she can contact him.

Barbara had learned a hard lesson about forgiveness and reconciliation: you can't wait for the other guy to make the first move. I suspect her brother was too ashamed of his actions to ever think she could forgive him, so he kept his distance for a while and then dropped out of sight. By the time Barbara's heart had softened toward him, it was too late.

But even in situations where your offender—or a person you have offended—is still a part of your everyday life, you need to accept the fact that it's probably going to be up to you to begin the healing process. After all, you're the one reading a book on forgiveness, so the concept is apparently one you've been thinking about. That puts the ball in your court. Once you begin to get the first inkling that you need to forgive someone, or ask for forgiveness from someone, that's probably a fairly good indication that you need to take the initiative.

I cannot begin to relate the countless stories of regret that I've heard from people who wish they had done something that they knew they should do at the time, before it was too late. Expecting someone else to get the message about forgiveness isn't exactly something you can count on. Look around you; television shows, commercials, movies, and music frequently

> Only the one who has been hurt can bring healing. The other person cannot. It is the one who has been hurt who has to be willing to be hurt again to show love, if there is to be hope that healing will come.
>
> —FRANCIS SCHAEFFER

Forgiveness is the healing of wounds caused by another. You choose to let go of a past wrong and no longer be hurt by it. Forgiveness is a strong move to make, like turning your shoulders sideways to walk quickly on a crowded sidewalk. It's your move.

—GORDON ATKINSON

sound out a message of revenge, not forgiveness. It's not impossible to find the inspiration to forgive, but there are an awful lot of messages out there trying to convince us that we need to get the upper hand on our offenders. The chance that someone will stumble on a message about forgiveness—a message powerful enough to penetrate their heart—is just that. A chance.

Don't take that chance. If you have offended someone and you want to ask their forgiveness, don't put it off. Barbara realized that too late; she never confronted her brother about the possibility that he'd been drinking again before she abruptly threw him out. She wanted—needed—his forgiveness for that. She may never get it now.

Likewise, she wanted to let him know that she had forgiven him for stealing from her. Most of all, though, she wanted to be reconciled with him. There's always the possibility, of course, that he would have rejected her, but at least she would have had peace in knowing she had tried. Living with that kind of regret is particularly painful; our sins of omission often cause more suffering than our sins of commission do.

"There are many persons ready to do what is right because in their hearts they know it is right. But they hesitate, waiting for the other fellow to make the make the first move—and he, in turn, waits for you," Marian Anderson points out.[2] If you are ready to do what in your heart you know is right, don't wait for the other guy. To him, you are the other guy—and he's waiting for you to make the first move.

REFLECTION

Think about what it is that holds you back from doing what is right. Consider all the possibilities: fear, pride, uncertainty, shame, embarrassment, and so forth. The fear of rejection is an especially powerful deterrent when it comes to forgiveness and reconciliation, for example. How can you get past those factors in order to take the initiative you know you should take?

PRACTICE

Make a list of every situation in your life in which you are waiting for someone else to make the first move. It doesn't have to be related to forgiveness or reconciliation. Maybe it's another couple's turn to have you and your spouse over for dinner. Who cares whose turn it is? If you want to get together with them, invite them back to your house for dinner. We often don't realize the pleasure we deprive ourselves of—all because we're waiting for someone else to take the initiative.

> Resentment is one burden that is incompatible with your success. Always be the first to forgive; and forgive yourself first always.
>
> **—DAN ZADRA**

13

4 Be Immediate

People who have learned to develop a healthy sense of humor in order to get through life figure out pretty early on that they also need to develop a finely tuned sense of where the line is that they should never cross. Humor can be hurtful to others—and embarrassing to everyone—when you're on such a roll that you ignore all the flashing warning signs indicating that you've gone too far or that you never should have put your perpetual joking machine into motion in the first place. On occasions when you somehow resisted the temptation to say something that you thought was funny and quickly realized how inappropriate your remark would have been, you have to believe that there really is a God who is powerful enough to shut your mouth for you.

One such occasion stands out in my mind like no other. A glance at caller ID told me one of my brothers—who hadn't called me in years, if not decades—was at the other end of the ringing telephone. My first impulse was to answer with some witty but wickedly sarcastic remark, but when I opened my mouth, all I said was "Hello." Weird—whatever that long-forgotten one-liner was, I'm sure it was a good one.

For the next few minutes, my brother choked back the tears as he tried to tell me how sorry he was that he had not kept in touch over the years or let me know how much he loved me and cared about me. "Will … you … forgive me?" he finally asked, slowly and painfully.

Moved as I was by his confession, a part of me still—*still*—felt like joking around. The perfect comeback formed in my mind (something having to do with groveling on his part, I suspect), but what came out of my mouth—and my heart—was this: "Of course I forgive you. I love you. I will always love you, and nothing will ever change that."

I've long held to a theory that among the many everyday miracles that the Spirit of God works are these two:

Scenario one: We say something completely inane to someone who needs to hear something completely profound, and the Spirit of God catches our words, repairs them or massages them or does whatever it is the Spirit does, and transforms them into the very words the other person needed to hear. We speak Homer Simpson; the person in need hears Mother Teresa. Sometimes, God simply refuses to allow others to suffer our stupidity.

Scenario two: We think of something completely inane that we *intend* to say to someone who needs to hear something completely profound, and the Spirit of God goes to work on our thoughts before we ever give voice to them. This is one of those

> A wise man will make haste to forgive, because he knows the full value of time and will not suffer it to pass away in unnecessary pain.
>
> **—SAMUEL JOHNSON**

acts of God for which we should lie facedown on the floor for days in deep and abiding gratitude.

That's what I felt like doing after that phone call, and here's why: when he regained his composure, my brother told me he had prayed a very specific prayer before he dialed my number. He said he wasn't sure God could ever forgive him or ever love him, so he had prayed, "God, the first thing Marcia says when I ask her forgiveness, I'm going to take as coming from you too. If she forgives me immediately, I'll finally believe that you will also forgive me."

Dear God in heaven! I nearly sank to my knees when my brother told me that. My mind whirred with the enormous responsibility he had placed on me. What if I had launched into a three-minute "No way, José" stand-up routine? Or worse, what if I had put the jokes aside and slipped into lecture mode, pausing for an oh-so-superior moment before taking a deep breath and telling him that, yes, it was high time he owned up to his negligence and disregard for my feelings?

Look again at the words he heard instead—words that he believed came straight from the heart of God: "Of course I forgive you. I love you. I will always love you, and nothing will ever change that." God forgave him. God loved him. God would always love him. Nothing would ever change God's love for him.

We know our words can have incredibly serious repercussions. But so can our silence, our hesitation, our dramatic pause for effect—our tone of voice once we design to extend our forgiveness to a mere mortal. I recall one incident in particular when I was on the receiving end of that kind of "forgiveness";

Forgiveness is the great yes. Acting in accordance with the highest ideals of our tradition, I do not have a choice of whether I *should* forgive you, but whether or not I *will*. And I must if I want to be alive.

—Martin Buber

16

my friend's lengthy pause, followed by an exaggerated sigh, told me she intended to make me twist in the wind and thereby teach me a lesson before she would condescend to forgive me. That's not forgiveness; that's meanness.

Whenever possible—whenever we know deep down that we can genuinely forgive an offender who has sought our forgiveness in true humility—we need to extend our forgiveness without hesitation. Our slightest pause can communicate a message we never intended—uncertainty, reluctance, even insincerity. Forgiveness is too important a gift to be withheld even momentarily.

Reflection

Has anyone ever made you twist in the wind? If so, you know how demeaning their attitude was. Now be honest: Have you ever made someone else twist in the wind for a while before you gave in and forgave her or accepted her apology? If so, you now know how condescending you appeared to her. I suspect it's probably time you apologized for that. Bluntness can be a big help in getting you through such a humbling experience: "You know, I was a real jerk back when you apologized to me for _____. I should have forgiven you immediately, but no. I just had to try to make you sweat for a while. I cannot believe how rotten that was. I am so sorry I ever treated you that way. Will you forgive me? Oh, and I'll understand completely if you don't answer right away."

Be even-tempered, content with second place, quick to forgive an offense. Forgive as quickly and completely as the Master forgave you.

—**Colossians 3:13**
(The Message)

17

PRACTICE

Here's one way you can practice immediate forgiveness so you'll be better prepared when a real opportunity comes along. If you're like me, your blood often reaches a boiling point as you read the newspaper or listen to the nightly news. Maybe it's a political issue that gets you riled up, and you become particularly incensed at those who muddy the issue with false information or deceptive tactics. Your head fills up with one comeback after another, all those things you'd like to say if you were face-to-face with that scurrilous politician or inept expert or ignorant spokesperson. Perfect opportunity to practice forgiveness! There's no way you can do it in person, so it's risk-free. You can immediately and without humiliation forgive the talking head. (I have to do this way too often with fellow journalists that I thankfully will never meet; I mentally forgive them for being such a blight on a profession I hold so dear.)

Whoever is devoid of the power to forgive is devoid of the power to love.

—MARTIN LUTHER KING JR.

Activist Anger

5

It's been some twenty-five years since I met a young woman I'll call Sylvia. At the time, she worked with the National Council of Churches on a project to promote breastfeeding or provide infant formula or purify the water for mixing powdered formula—I've long since forgotten her exact focus—for women in what were then called Third World countries. Though I can't for the life of me remember specifically what her mission was, I will never forget the intensity of it. Every big and little aspect of her life in some way related to that mission. And every person she met, me included, was in some way responsible for the plight of these women whose babies were dying.

As important as her mission was, her anger and hostility toward just about everyone who didn't share her single-minded focus caused more people to ignore her cause than contribute to it. After spending a couple of hours with her, I came to one irreversible conclusion: I wouldn't make a very good activist. Since I had long known I wouldn't be very good at partisan politics or choosing sides across the liberal-conservative divide, that pretty much reduced my future options by two or three, depending on who's doing the counting.

My feeling at the time was this: from what I'd seen of activists, political partisans, and the like, they weren't exactly a forgiving lot. Over the years, of course, that notion has been challenged any number of times. And I've had to confront my own penchant for unforgiveness more times than I care to admit. Unfortunately, though, my initial assessment stands, and recent events bear this out.

For instance, we see the ongoing conflict in the Episcopal Church over homosexuality, the authority of the Bible, and the legitimacy of church policy. The future of the church itself is at stake. But what concerns me more than anything is the anger and hostility and intolerance I've witnessed as this controversy has run its course. Oh, and I don't mean intolerance toward gays. I mean intolerance toward each other. The anger and hostility and intolerance I'm talking about has been directed by Christians against Christians. And yet, week after week, Christians join hands and pray the Lord's Prayer, failing to recognize the disconnect between their words and their actions.

We've seen parents forgive the very people who took the lives of their children, survivors forgive murderous terrorists, rape victims forgive their attackers. High-profile victims like missionary Gracia Burnham openly and genuinely forgive militant abductors and cold-blooded killers. But people of faith on opposite sides of a supercharged issue like abortion or homosexuality for some reason find it difficult to forgive one another.

What does the Lord require of you but to do justice and to love kindness and to walk humbly with your God?

—MICAH 6:8 (NRSV)

20

Or consider the war in Iraq. I recently heard a Washington observer say that in her thirty years as a political insider, she has never seen the level of bitterness that has pervaded the capital, and the country, in the aftermath of the war. Bitterness stems from an inability to forgive, and the inability to forgive prevents the kind of bipartisan cooperation it's going to take to solve the very real and immediate problems our nation is facing.

And I don't just mean a one-time expression of forgiveness. I suspect that if two individuals on opposite sides of the abortion debate, for example, felt the need to ask each other's forgiveness, each one would eventually extend it. Likewise, two political adversaries might find that they actually like each other as human beings and grant forgiveness as well. What is sorely needed, though, is for all of us to cultivate a lifestyle of forgiveness toward entire groups of people—not compromising on our convictions, not backing down on what we believe to be right, but living in an attitude of ongoing forgiveness toward each other.

It's not enough to point to the many times we have forgiven others, even those who continue to hurt us. Forgiving your spouse for being insensitive to your needs does not cancel out the necessity of forgiving all those dastardly Democrats or Republicans, pro-abortionists or anti-abortionists, pro-gays or anti-gays. Try as we might to get around it, there's simply no such thing as partial forgiveness in the kingdom of God.

It gets harder, of course, especially when we get to the point of figuring out why we resist forgiving others. Any

> If you hate a person, you hate something in him that is part of yourself.
>
> —HERMAN HESSE

21

good counselor has the answer to that: We find it hardest to forgive in others the character flaws we see in ourselves. Your militancy exposes my militancy; your intolerance reveals my intolerance; your judgmentalism reflects my judgmentalism; your pride mirrors my pride. Not a pretty picture, but an accurate one.

But seeing ourselves in that not-so-pretty picture is exactly what it takes to cultivate forgiveness toward the opposition. When we feel passionately about an injustice or sin or any one of a host of theologically and socially controversial issues—and are tempted to take an unforgiving stand against those who disagree—that's when we are most in need of understanding our own character flaws. If your narrow-mindedness makes me seethe, you can be pretty sure that I have a few narrow pathways in my own mind.

It's never easy to take a hard look at ourselves. We want so much to believe that not only are we right, but we are also better—better than others, better than we used to be, better at reaching those right conclusions that we cling to so tenaciously. But forgiving others becomes so much easier when we realize that those others aren't all that different from us—or maybe better, that we aren't all that different from them.

We can be passionate about a cause without causing strife. We can fight for what we believe in without fighting people. We can work toward eradicating injustice without treating others unjustly. It just takes a little face time—with our own image.

> Forgiveness is the act of admitting we are like other people.
>
> —CHRISTINA BALDWIN

REFLECTION

Take a good, hard look at yourself. Not literally, of course, unless you think it would help. Spend some time in self-reflection by reflecting first on what it is about your opposition that bugs you the most. Let's suppose that your congregation is embroiled in that age-old conflict that has torn many a house of worship asunder: deciding on the color of the carpet. You and your buddies want blue; your opponent and his cronies want red. (This has nothing to do with states' voting colors. Honest.) You are absolutely certain that blue is exactly the color God wants that carpet to be, and you cannot believe that this other renegade group is being so stubborn about it. *Red?* How can they keep insisting that God prefers *red*? They're just being difficult, that's all there is to it.

Stubborn. Insistent. Difficult. Three words that just may require a bit of reflection.

PRACTICE

Most of the issues that we become so incensed about are complex problems that defy simplistic solutions. We're so quick to offer our opinions on how a wrong can be made right, but the truth is, we each have a very limited perspective on any given situation. We need the help of someone with a much broader perspective. That would be God.

If we seek to understand and forgive, we must forget our own expectations and assumptions, encountering others as they are at a particular moment. In meeting others and ourselves "where they/we are," we follow God's example in the Ishmael story, finding hope and opportunity in places and times that otherwise might be filled with hopelessness and despair.

—RABBI RAMI SHAPIRO

23

Level your activist anger at God. Whatever it is that makes you gnash your teeth and tear your hair out, let God know all about it. Don't even think about leaving anything out. Get it all out of your system and dump it on God, who clearly can take it. Trust God to give us the wisdom to solve our otherwise unsolvable problems. And then ask the Spirit of God to give you the grace to forgive those whose beliefs and opinions run counter to your own.

Initiative is doing the right thing without being told.

—VICTOR HUGO

Exercise Your Humility

One of the glib expressions people often use today is this one: "It's easier to ask forgiveness than permission." I cringe every time I hear that, for several reasons, the first of which has nothing to do with forgiveness. That's the element of deception implied in the statement. Whatever the thing is that you want to do, you know you should ask for permission first but instead you choose to be devious and do it anyway.

Even worse, though, is the implication that somehow asking for forgiveness is easy. Easy? I think not. That kind of thinking betrays a shallow understanding of the humbling but ultimately powerful act of seeking forgiveness. I can only assume that the act that needed permission was little more than a misdemeanor requiring a sheepish, "Aw, shucks" request for permission. Such a cavalier attitude toward forgiveness cheapens a priceless concept.

The Jewish and Christian traditions share a basic understanding about the nature of authentically seeking forgiveness from God and others: it requires a heavy dose of humility. Nowhere in the Scriptures of these two great faith traditions do you detect a flippant attitude when forgiveness is sought or extended. In fact, in Jewish tradition, an entire day is given over to exploring, asking for, and receiving forgiveness. On Yom Kippur (or Day of Atonement), which lasts from sunset to sunset, Jews are called to abstain from eating and drinking and to attend services in synagogue, where they confess their sins as a community.

On at least one occasion in the Bible, the need for undeserved forgiveness rendered the offenders speechless. The story of Joseph is found in chapters 37 through 45 of the book of Genesis, and if you haven't read it in a while—or if all you remember of it is Joseph's "coat of many colors" from your Bible lessons as a child—you may want to go back and re-read it. It has all the elements of a really good novel, including the obligatory seduction scene.

Anyway, back to forgiveness. The situation is this: Joseph, one of the twelve sons of Jacob, had been betrayed by his brothers in Canaan and sold into slavery, ending up in Egypt. Eventually, he becomes the pharaoh's right-hand man, his most trusted aide, and takes charge of distributing Egypt's surplus food to Canaanites suffering through a lengthy famine. Among the Canaanites who come to him pleading for provisions are several of his brothers. They do not recognize Joseph, but he recognizes them. There's a whole lot more that happens at this point, but we'll fast-forward to a subsequent visit when Joseph decides to reveal his identity to his brothers.

> God resists the proud, but gives grace to the humble.
>
> **—1 Peter 5:5 (NKJV)**

Now at this point, Joseph is overcome with emotion at the prospect of this imminent reunion with his brothers and eventual reunion with his father. The brothers, however, are overcome with a different kind of emotion—shame. Oh, and fear. When Joseph reveals who he is and asks if Jacob is still alive, his brothers cannot utter a single word. They're in shock, pure and simple. Joseph immediately assures them that he means them no harm; before they even have an opportunity to beg his forgiveness, Joseph grants it. He turns the focus away from their treachery and toward God's goodness. You may have thought you were punishing me, he tells them, but look what happened—God put me in a position to save your lives!

I don't know about you, but I'd say that's a fairly healthy response to betrayal.

I love the story of Joseph. I love the way the story brings God's work out from behind the scenes and places it front and center. I love the way he forgives his brothers so completely and the way he lavishes the riches of the kingdom on them. And I love the way he embraces them with sheer joy. Joy! Yes, that's another by-product of a lifestyle of forgiveness.

But back to humility and its negative counterpart, pride. Humility is an absolutely essential ingredient in both the seeking and the granting of forgiveness; pride is an absolute impediment to both as well. Humility softens our hearts and prepares us to request for ourselves that which we don't deserve or to grant to another that which he does not deserve. Pride hardens our hearts and insists that we neither are in need of forgiveness nor are obligated to offer it.

Jesus said, "Whoever humbles himself as this little child is the greatest in the kingdom of heaven."

—MATTHEW 18:4
(NKJV)

Look again at the story of Joseph. If anyone had legitimate cause to be proud and arrogant, it was Joseph himself. Rejected, abandoned, enslaved, falsely accused, unjustly imprisoned, and forgotten for years, he later rose to the second-highest governmental position in Egypt. Equipped with nearly unlimited power and authority, he could have dug in his heels and made his brothers die of starvation by withholding the grain that would have saved them. Or if a slow death was not to his liking, he could have simply had them executed.

Despite the enormous amount of power he possessed, he humbled himself before his siblings. He knew that his earthly power paled in comparison to the spiritual power of forgiveness and reconciliation.

REFLECTION

Pride can be one of the most insidious flaws in our character due to its uncanny ability to blind us to its very existence. We're more apt to be aware of our dishonesty or manipulation or unfaithfulness than of our pride. We need help to root out those prideful areas that are all too often hidden to us but are evident to others. We can either live in denial that pride is a problem for us or we can ask God to expose our pride so we can finally deal with it. Trust me, that first option may look appealing, but sooner or later some other mortal is going to bring you up short by pointing out what an arrogant so-and-so you are, and that's never fun. It's much better to humble

Humility is not a grace that can be acquired in a few months. It is the work of a lifetime.

—FRANÇOIS FÉNELON

yourself before God and ask the Spirit to illuminate the dark corners of your nature where you've allowed pride to lurk for far too long. If you make that request known to God today, there's a fair-to-middling chance that you're going to be pretty miserable for the next few days. Because no matter how gentle the Spirit is in exposing your pride, it still makes for an awfully ugly picture. But then you get the payoff—a heightened awareness of those areas of your life that you need to work on and an enormous amount of help from God to make that work effective. What's a couple of days of misery compared to a less arrogant future? I'd say the payoff far exceeds the investment.

PRACTICE

Choose one day this week to focus on humility. Decide that on this one day, you will capture every prideful thought (and temptation) and turn it into a humble action. Let's say a colleague criticizes your work, and your nose gets decidedly out of joint. Put your nose back in its place and ask God to show you—quickly—how to respond from a place of humility. You may find yourself thanking your colleague for pointing out a problem you need to fix. Or not. In any event, you'll probably succeed in deflating the attitude of your colleague, who's likely to be all puffed up with her own pride and fully expecting a fight from you, which you've just denied her. Ten big points for you! Not that we're keeping score or anything.

> What makes humility so desirable is the marvelous thing it does to us; it creates in us a capacity for the closest possible intimacy with God.
>
> —MONICA BALDWIN

Continue to look for evidence of humility in all your interactions with others and in the interactions among others that you witness—at work, in a store, as you're driving. Sometimes we discover humility in the most unlikely places. I once heard a physician tell a patient that he had no idea why she was getting better, that her improvement had to be the work of a power much higher than the medical community or pharmaceutical industry. Now *that's* humility!

At the end of the day, make a journal entry about each indication of humility that you witnessed or experienced for yourself. Be sure to include elements like facial expressions and gestures. Then read over what you wrote, and see what you can learn about humbling yourself. Ask questions like these: Did the people who exhibited true humility seem weak or degraded in any way by their actions? Were other people in any way affected by these acts of humility? Be honest; sometimes when we humble ourselves before others, there is no visible effect whatsoever on those "others." By examining incidents where humility is exhibited, we can be better prepared for the consequences of our own acts of humility. There may not always be an immediate payoff. We need to remember to continue practicing humility regardless of the other person's reaction.

The only true forgiveness is that which is offered and extended even before the offender has apologized and sought it.

—SØREN KIERKEGAARD

The Grace to Forgive

Throughout my formative years, all I ever knew about grace I learned at the supper table. Somebody's supper table that is, not our family's. I suppose we said grace on Thanksgiving and at random times when our Sunday school lessons spilled over to the kitchen, but beyond that, the word *grace* was nothing more than the name of the princess of Monaco, one of my mother's favorite actresses—Grace Kelly, for those too young to remember.

Even after my faith and I had matured a bit, I admit to having a shallow understanding of the concept of grace. I understood that it was a gift from God, something that gave us the ability or capacity to live the way God wants us to. It was more than that, but I never really had a good handle on what that was. I still can't offer an adequate verbal definition of grace, but today I have a stockpile of examples of how grace has operated in my life.

Each time you think of [a painful past experience], worry at it, feel bad about it or mad, you are expending energy, you are forking over grace units into a dark void, like throwing money out a window. If you examine each and every one of these issues, you will find a remarkable similarity— each one can be resolved by forgiveness.

—CAROLYN MYSS

The latest involved a two-month stint as a caregiver for a longtime friend and cancer patient. The way I see it, I got up one morning, left my family in Florida, flew to Colorado, and did what I was supposed to do for the next eight weeks. It wasn't much, really—driving Alice to medical treatments, running errands, making sure she ate right, drank enough fluids, and took her medication, and assorted similar responsibilities.

Well, you'd think I had sacrificed my life, my limbs, and my firstborn child judging by the way some people reacted when they found out what I had done. But no matter what they said, it just didn't feel like a big deal at all. Even in retrospect, I can't honestly say that it was all that difficult. In fact, one of the words that comes to mind most often when I think of that experience is "seamless." I seamlessly went from my own home and family, became fully integrated into Alice's home and family life, and returned to my own home and family as if that whole process was a normal part of everyone's life.

Try as I might, I can't make it into anything more than that. And that's where the word *grace* comes in. God gave two families the grace to take a two-month side trip that appeared to outside observers as if it was a detour over rough and rocky terrain, when in fact it proved to be a very smooth ride that in many ways benefited everyone involved.

As the concept of grace was operating in my life on a practical level, a deeper insight into grace was revealed to me on a much higher level—literally. At 14,110 feet, in fact. Atop Pikes Peak near Colorado Springs.

It was there that Katherine Lee Bates began writing the poem that eventually became the lyrics to "America, the Beautiful." Now I could go on and on about the breathtaking view that inspired those lyrics, but I promise I won't. I will say this, though: I will never again be able to hear that song without welling up at the line "God shed his grace on thee." Because standing there at the summit, looking out over the city, thinking about Alice eight thousand feet below and my family two thousand miles to the east, I understood for the first time that God really does "shed" his grace on us.

What an inspired image that word evokes! God sheds his grace, letting it fall on us when we need it the most, transforming the unnatural into the most natural thing in the world, and giving us power we couldn't possibly have otherwise. It's as if God says, "I have more than enough grace of my own. Here, let me shower you with some. You look as if you could use it."

Sometimes God does just that. The Spirit showers us with grace before we realize we need it or even think to ask for it. At other times, though, it seems as if we do need to ask for it. Since I'm not God, I don't exactly know why that is, but I suspect it has something to do with humbling ourselves. It usually does.

Which brings us back to forgiveness. If you've ever said something like "I could never forgive him!" then you're probably right about that. You could never, in your own power, forgive your offender. But God's grace can and will empower you to extend forgiveness to even the most heinous person you know. How else can you explain—or understand—news stories about a hit-and-run victim who forgives the driver who left him

> Grace does not make everything right.... Grace is rather an amazing power to look earthy reality full in the face, see its sad and tragic edges, feel its cruel cuts, join in the primeval chorus against its outrageous unfairness, and yet feel in your deepest being that it is good and right for you to be alive on God's good earth.
>
> —LEWIS B. SMEDES

33

to die, or parents who forgive their child's murderer, or a frail, elderly woman who forgives the monster who repeatedly raped her? You can't explain it on a human level, nor can you understand it. The only explanation is God's grace. God shed his grace on them, whether they asked for it or not, whether they understood it or not, whether they even believe in God or not.

I'm guessing it would take a lifetime or two to get a really good handle on grace, because it's a concept so foreign to human nature that we can hardly wrap our minds around it. But that doesn't mean we shouldn't try to grasp it. Or that we shouldn't ask for it.

REFLECTION

Be thankful for the gift of grace. Not just the grace that the Spirit has bestowed on you, but also on the capacity you have for bestowing grace on others. Recall an incident or a time when the gift of grace was clearly operating in your life. Prayerfully express gratitude for every detail you can remember. A prayerful meditation on my time with Alice, for example, might include such things as the grace God gave Alice's daughters to accept a virtual stranger coming into their lives so abruptly and for so long, and the grace it took for my own family to handle my prolonged absence. Reciting the evidences of grace in your life is no empty gesture; rather, it's a meaningful endeavor that leads to a revelation of the abundance of grace that God has lavished on you.

Sunrise breaks through the darkness for good people—God's grace and mercy and justice!
—**PSALM 112:4**
(THE MESSAGE)

PRACTICE

Theologians often define grace as God's unmerited favor. Demonstrate this understanding of the concept of grace in some way in your everyday life this week. Bestow your unmerited favor on someone who has done nothing to earn it. Excuse an egregious error an embarrassed employee has made. Suspend the expected punishment for a disobedient but repentant child. Perform an unanticipated act of kindness when your spouse really botches things up. These small expressions of grace prepare you to more readily respond in a gracious way when undeserved forgiveness is warranted.

All major religious traditions carry basically the same message, that is love, compassion and forgiveness ... the important thing is they should be part of our daily lives.

—THE DALAI LAMA

8 Cultivating Compassion

Too often the stories we hear on the news or read about in the daily paper are so appalling that we can hardly believe that they're actually true. And once in a great while, a story describes a crime so horrifying that we can hardly believe that the offender is actually human.

That was the case in October 2001, when a young woman named Chante Mallard got behind the wheel of her car after a night of heavy drinking and drug use. Her car struck a man walking along the side of the road, and Mallard left the scene of the accident.

But this was no simple hit-and-run. Mallard left the scene with the victim embedded in her shattered windshield. Gregory Biggs lived long enough to plead with her to call for help after she hid the car in her garage. Instead, the young woman went in her house and "entertained" her boyfriend; some time later she and some friends dumped Biggs's body in a park. Now known as the "Windshield Murderer," Mallard was sentenced to fifty years in prison for her crime.

But even before her sentencing, Biggs's son Brandon, then a high school student, had extended his forgiveness to her after working through his loss and the initial hatred he felt toward her. In a number of media interviews, he specifically expressed compassion for her and her family.

Compassion—that's a word that permeates the Hebrew and Christian Scriptures, but somehow we Jews and Christians have for the most part failed to acquire a solid reputation as compassionate people. Oh, we have our moments, and thankfully, we have other positive qualities that people generally associate with us. But the honor of being closely identified with compassion goes instead to Buddhists, who have transformed the word into a lifestyle. "Compassion is wisdom that directly benefits others," writes former Buddhist monk Christopher Titmuss. To some Buddhists, that idea is signified by the image of a large bird soaring through the air, one wing representing compassion and the other wisdom.[3]

Compassion in its purest form benefits others in that it involves sharing in the suffering of another person, in the suffering of your offender, in the sufferings of all people. Today the phrase "I feel your pain" may have degenerated into an expression of mockery, but its literal sense describes exactly what compassion is. We feel another person's pain so acutely that we are moved to do what we can to relieve it.

That's what Marietta Jaeger experienced following the kidnapping and murder of her young daughter. Much to her own

In this moral universe nothing is useless. The sighs and groans of the persecuted and tortured, the courage and fidelity of the unremarked, the generosities and compassion that happen unsung, the heroisms often hidden—these do not just evaporate into the ether. No, they impregnate the atmosphere.

—DESMOND TUTU

surprise, she began to feel compassionate toward the murderer and his family after admitting to God that she was finally willing to forgive the man. She even offered to help him, pleading during the trial that he be spared the death penalty and reaching out to his mother after he committed suicide in prison.

That kind of compassion can't be faked. Jaeger and her family had been devastated by the loss of their daughter. For more than a year, they did not know what had happened to her. The agony they endured was nothing short of torturous, and what Jaeger wanted most was nothing short of heavy-duty revenge.

But no sooner had Jaeger confessed that she wanted to kill the abductor—at the time, she still held out hope that the little girl was alive—than she realized deep down she would have to forgive him. Eventually, she also realized that to have compassion on the kidnapper was to honor her daughter—and that to wish him dead in her name was to dishonor her daughter.

For Brandon Biggs and Marietta Jaeger, compassion came at a high cost. Theirs were no superficial attempts at being do-gooders or acting religious. The compassion in their lives sank so deep into their spirits that it would have been impossible to eradicate it, impossible to trivialize it, impossible to deny it.

Biggs's story, by the way, didn't end with Mallard's sentencing. After writing about his experience in "Compassion," a newsletter produced by death-row inmates, Biggs, now a seminary student, was awarded a $10,000 scholarship—every penny of it raised by those same inmates. All he wanted was to share God's love, mercy, and forgiveness with one woman who desperately needed it, but he touched countless prisoners in the

For me, forgiveness and compassion are always linked: how do we hold people accountable for wrongdoing and yet at the same time remain in touch with their humanity enough to believe in their capacity to be transformed?

—**BELL HOOKS**

process. And they, in turn, touched his life in a tangible way out of gratitude for his kindness and courage.

Joseph Campbell, author of the wonderful *Hero with a Thousand Faces* and many other books, writes that compassion so immerses you in the suffering of another that you "forget yourself and … do what is necessary."[4] We need to forget ourselves—and I repeat: we need to *forget* ourselves—and do what is necessary to restore the lives of broken people. That may or may not mean serving them in practical ways, as Jaeger did, but it does mean forgiving them. One thing is certain: a compassionate person is a forgiving person; he simply can't help it.

REFLECTION

Examine your life with respect to the manner in which you serve others or the extent to which you serve others. What drives that service? Are you moved by compassion to help the broken, the hurting, the needy? If not, why not? Don't judge yourself; just think about that question with something of a detached curiosity. (I once wondered the very same thing about myself, and the conclusion I reached was that I had been unwilling to forget myself, which is no doubt why I repeated that phrase earlier.) Maybe you serve other people a great deal, but your work on their behalf is driven by something other than compassion. Any number of factors can come into play: guilt, the need for praise, a sense of obligation. Regardless of the conclusions you draw during this time of reflection, end by

By forgiving we enhance the presence of compassion in the world.

—RABBI DAVID WOLPE

Compassion is the feeling of shared suffering. When you understand that you aren't alone in your suffering, there is the birth of love. When there is love there is the opportunity for peace.

—DEEPAK CHOPRA

praying and asking God for a greater measure of compassion toward others—and especially toward anyone you know you need to forgive.

PRACTICE

Clothe yourselves with compassion, kindness, humility, gentleness and patience. Bear with each other and forgive whatever grievances you may have against one another. Forgive as the Lord forgave you.

—COLOSSIANS 3:12–14
(NIV)

The parable of the good Samaritan offers a compelling illustration of compassion. Maybe you haven't read it since your Sunday school days, or if you are part of another faith tradition, maybe you have never read it at all. It's found in Luke 10:30–37, and it's well worth reading. (It helps to know that the Samaritans were a mixed-race people who were looked down upon at the time of Jesus.)

9 Harvesting Forgiveness

Back in the heyday of televangelism, before one scandal after another rocked the ministries of a number of prominent evangelists, a lot of unsuspecting viewers bought into one great big fat lie: if you gave your money and other resources to this or that ministry, God would be *required* to reward you in return—and in like manner. Give a million dollars to Reverend Billy Bob's broadcast, and God *had to* give back to you a million dollars or more. In some sermons, much more—threefold, sevenfold, or tenfold, depending on who was doing the divine calculations.

Unsuspecting viewers, of course, still buy into that lie, because it's still proclaimed throughout the land and beyond. The sad thing—well, other than the fact that lots of people lost the farm and the faith they had once cherished even as those dastardly televangelists continued to bilk hundreds of thousands of followers out of their money and their trust in other people, all in the name of God, but don't get me started on that or I may start to use such strong language that I'd have to beg your forgiveness and God's as well—the sad thing is that the televangelists' distorted teaching is based on a sound biblical and life principle. Some know it as the principle of sowing and reaping; others call it the law of cause and effect.

As usual, *The Message*, a Bible paraphrase by Eugene Peterson, expresses this principle in blunt language:

> Don't be misled. No one makes a fool of God. What a person plants, he will harvest. The person who plants selfishness, ignoring the needs of others—ignoring God!—harvests a crop of weeds. All he'll have to show for his life is weeds! But the one who plants in response to God, letting God's Spirit do the growth work in him, harvests a crop of real life, eternal life. (Gal. 6:7–8)

Like any principle, this one can be misrepresented, altered, even interfered with. But that doesn't invalidate its truth. And the truth for us is that if we sow forgiveness, we will reap forgiveness. The Scriptures are clear on this point.

On one occasion, Jesus tells his disciples that what they ask for in prayer will be given to them if they truly believe. But then he adds this: "Whenever you stand praying, forgive, if you have anything against anyone; so that your Father in heaven may also forgive you your trespasses" (Mark 11:25–26, NRSV).

Whenever you pray. The way I read this, it really doesn't matter what else you are praying about. You could be praying for a

Sow everywhere the good seed given to you. Sow in good ground, sow in sand, sow among the stones, sow on the road, sow among the weeds. Perhaps some of these seeds will open up and grow and bring forth fruit, even if not at once.

—Nineteenth-century Russian monk Seraphim of Sarov

friend's healing or praising God for his overwhelming good-ness or railing at God for ignoring you completely, not that I know anyone who would ever do that or anything, and you're supposed to stop and let God know that you forgive Osama Bin Laden for being such a well-hidden madman, or else God won't be all that inclined to forgive you for yelling at him to try to get his attention.

Anyway, in the Sermon on the Mount, Jesus expresses this principle in even stronger terms: "If you forgive others their trespasses, your heavenly Father will also forgive you; but if you do not forgive others, neither will your Father forgive your trespasses" (Matt. 6:14–15, NRSV). Theologians puzzle over that last verse: Isn't God's forgiveness supposed to be predi-cated on repentance only? If we completely forget to forgive someone we should have forgiven, does that nullify God's for-giveness? And what's up with his petulant attitude?

Theological quandaries aside, the principle remains intact. Sow forgiveness and you will reap forgiveness; sow unforgive-ness and you will reap unforgiveness.

But how does this work in our daily lives? I can tell you one way straight off, and it's based on the idea that like attracts like. A person with an unforgiving spirit acts like a magnet for other people with unforgiving spirits; they'll fuel your bitterness and anger and resentment like nothing else can. At first you may find some consolation in their validation of your justified anger, but heaven help you if you ever do anything to offend them. Remember? They have unforgiving spirits.

> Forgiveness is the highest, most beautiful form of love. In return, you will receive untold peace and happiness.
>
> —ROBERT MULLER

Christ stated emphatically that it was quite impossible, in the nature of things, for a man to be at peace with God and at variance with his neighbor. This disquieting fact is often hushed up, but it is undeniable that Christ said it, and the truth of it is enshrined in the petition for forgiveness in the "Lord's Prayer."

—J. B. Phillips

In the same way, a person with a forgiving spirit can't help but attract the attention, respect, and friendship of other people with forgiving spirits. They're the ones who recognize your efforts at sowing forgiveness, and it's from them that you will be most likely to reap immediate forgiveness whenever you need it. Wouldn't you rather surround yourself with forgiving people? Given my penchant for doing and saying really dumb things that I end up having to apologize for, I can assure you that I have filled my quota of intimate friends with the most forgiving sort of people.

So go and scatter the seeds of forgiveness anywhere and everywhere you can. Sow forgiveness when a cashier opts for talking to a coworker over ringing up your order, when your neighbor's dog gets into your garbage cans for the third time in a week, when Congress dips its grubby little hands into your pocket once again to fund yet another program you oppose. Or even worse, when a network cancels the only intelligent show in all of TV land. Just who do they think they are, anyway?

When the harvest begins to come in—when you notice that your friends and enemies and even God are all a bit more forgiving toward you—remember the principle of sowing and reaping. Remember it, too, the next time a genuinely serious offense requires your forgiveness. It's okay to hold the seeds of forgiveness in your hands for a while longer in those tougher situations. Just remember the harvest: sowing forgiveness means reaping forgiveness.

REFLECTION

What have you been sowing lately? Think about that. What does that mean with regard to what you can expect to reap? (Me, I've been sowing frenzy, and I can assure you, the principle holds true. Frenzy is precisely what I've been reaping.) What would you like to be sowing? When do you plan to start?

PRACTICE

One of the most beautiful prayers I know of is one that can be prayed by people of any faith expression. It's attributed to St. Francis of Assisi, the same St. Francis who is appropriately memorialized throughout America in garden statuary, holding a bird in the palm of his hand. Pray this prayer daily, if necessary, until Francis's request truly becomes your own:

Lord, make me an instrument of thy peace. Where there is hatred, let me sow love. Where there is injury, pardon. Where there is doubt, faith. Where there is despair, hope. Where there is darkness, light. Where there is sadness, joy. O Divine Master, grant that I may not so much seek to be consoled as to console; to be understood, as to understand; to be loved, as to love; for it is in giving that we receive, it is in pardoning that we are pardoned, and it is in dying that we are born to eternal life.

The forgiving state of mind is a magnetic power for attracting good.

—CATHERINE PORTER

45

10

A Relentlessly Forgiving God

A comparative study of ancient religions makes one thing abundantly clear: the Jewish and Christian God trumps all those other deities when it comes to forgiveness. I mean, let's get real here. The petty little gods the Canaanites worshipped? About the best they could muster was the appearance that a decent harvest was their doing; they cared not a whit about the misery of an individual's interior life. And the Roman gods, along with their Greek and Norse counterparts, just wanted to be appeased. As long as the people performed the sacrifices and brought the offerings they demanded, the gods withheld their wrath.

The God of the Hebrew and Christian scriptures, by contrast, has been all about forgiveness ever since Adam and Eve blew it, way back in the garden. The early days of the Hebrews were one long roller-coaster ride of sin and forgiveness—turning away from God, repenting of their sin, receiving God's forgiveness, and living in restored relationship with God. The

Bible is replete with examples of the Israelites' rocky relationship with God, who never winked and looked the other way when they abandoned his teachings but who also never failed to extend to them his unwavering mercy and forgiveness.

And when it came to individuals—well, there was just no stopping God from lavishing forgiveness on the least deserving. Imagine how we would skewer a president who not only had an adulterous affair that resulted in pregnancy but also made sure that his lover's husband was sent to the front lines of war to assure that he would be killed. Oh, but not until after he was granted leave so he could go home and have sex with his wife so everyone would think the baby was the husband's and not the president's. How forgiving would we be? But God forgave King David for all that and more, and didn't even remove him from power. No impeachment, no trial, no political angst played out in the media of the day. In fact, God called David "a man after my own heart." Adulterer, cheat, deceiver, abuser, liar, and yet he ends up in God's good graces. Some serious shame and sorrow and penitence preceded his absolution, but still. David had it pretty good.

And look at Manasseh! This guy was worse than a villain in a Quentin Tarantino movie. Granted, he became king at the age of twelve, which I guess would set anyone up for a lifetime of abusing power. But Manasseh was Osama Bin Laden and Saddam Hussein and Idi Amin rolled into one gigantic and nasty piece of work. He was a cruel and bloody king who sacrificed his own children to idols and, as tradition has it, put the prophet Isaiah to death. The Bible indicates that he was so evil,

> We all arrive at your doorstep sooner or later, loaded with guilt, our sins too much for us—but you get rid of them once and for all.
>
> —PSALM 65:2–3
> (THE MESSAGE)

> He forgives your sins—every one. He heals your diseases—every one.... As far as sunrise is from sunset, he has separated us from our sins.
>
> —PSALM 103:3, 12
> (THE MESSAGE)

and he had been so successful at getting the kingdom of Judah to worship other gods, that people began to ignore God.

> But Manasseh led Judah and the citizens of Jerusalem off the beaten path into practices of evil exceeding even the evil of the pagan nations that God had earlier destroyed. When God spoke to Manasseh and his people about this, they ignored him. (2 Chron. 33:9–10, *The Message*)

You have to figure that at this point, God was thinking, "After all I've done for you! You think you can ignore me? I'll show you!" So God allowed the Assyrians to attack Judah and carry Manasseh off to captivity in Babylon, but not before they put a hook in his nose and shackled his feet. That's when Manasseh finally heard the wake-up call that God had been sounding for decades:

> Now that he was in trouble, he went to his knees in prayer asking for help—total repentance before the God of his ancestors. As he prayed, God was touched; God listened and brought him back to Jerusalem as king. That convinced Manasseh that God was in control. (2 Chron. 33:11–12, *The Message*)

I have to confess that as beautiful a picture of God's forgiveness as this is, I could get all bent out of shape over how quickly

---

We are to be both forgiven and forgiving people.

—DAVID BRONNERT

We must realize that God is against us when we are sinning; yet we dare trust that His gracious love reaches to us across the chasm which separates us from Him. When we understand His loving attitude and accept His grace, He releases His love in us.

—K. MORGAN EDWARDS

all this played out. One day Manasseh is a brute, and pretty much the next day God is all over him, forgiving him *as he prayed.* I would have demanded more than a pure heart, which God can apparently see and I can't. I would have demanded at least a little bitty shred of evidence that Manasseh was good to go. Then, *and only then,* would he be restored as king of Judah. But that's me and not God.

Ignoring for a moment my inclination toward petty tyranny, there's a lesson in these stories for all of us. No matter how rotten we think we are, how unforgivable, how unworthy, how contemptible, none of us is beyond the reach of God's love and forgiveness. Even if you had an affair and caused the death of your lover's spouse to cover up your infidelity; even if you slaughtered innocent people and led an entire nation astray; even if you sacrificed the lives of your own children.

God wrote the book on the sacred art of forgiveness. It's filled with evidences of mercy and grace and blessing on the whole lot of humanity—the good and the bad alike. God's forgiveness permeates the pages of Scripture—displayed through his relentless determination to remain in relationship with the people he loves.

> Most laws condemn the soul and pronounce sentence. The result of the law of my God is perfect. It condemns but forgives. It restores—more than abundantly—what it takes away.
>
> —JIM ELLIOT

REFLECTION

Draw a picture of God. I'm serious. This can be a highly reflective, meditative activity. Meditate on the image of God before you begin. Think as you're drawing: What does God look like in my life? What picture springs to mind the moment

I hear the word *God*? If I were to imagine God's character traits on two sides of a scale, which would tip the scale in my favor—God's judgment or God's forgiveness? God's condemnation or God's love? How you perceive God will in large part determine how you perceive forgiveness.

PRACTICE

Sin has become a dirty word in our society. "I've made some mistakes in my life," we say, equating an offense like adultery with choosing Bismarck as the capital of South Dakota on a multiple-choice quiz. A grievous offense against God and others is no mistake; it's the definition of that dastardly word *sin*. If that dastardly word is so problematic for you, at least replace it with something with a little gravitas—offense, transgression, wrongdoing. Then confess it all to God so you can enjoy the freedom of forgiveness and a restored relationship with the Spirit.

Forgiveness is always free. But that doesn't mean that confession is always easy. Sometimes it is hard. Incredibly hard. It is painful to admit our sins and entrust ourselves to God's care.

—ERWIN W. LUTZER

Forgiving Yourself

Union organizer Dolores Huerta was once quoted as asking this succinct question: "If you haven't forgiven yourself something, how can you forgive others?" Had I been anywhere in the vicinity when she said that, I would have been the one jumping up and down, both arms flailing about in the air, begging her to call on me to respond. I have the answer, and it's equally succinct: "Easily. Very, very easily."

My unscientific, statistically unreliable observation of many of my fellow Americans has convinced me that we are a peculiarly masochistic lot. Our penchant for introspection and self-criticism makes us especially unforgiving of ourselves. Given the choice, a lot of us would sooner forgive a serial killer for his heinous crimes than forgive ourselves for making an insensitive remark to a friend sometime in the last century. The reason is fairly obvious: we don't have to live with the serial killer.

There's another reason why we're unable, or at least reluctant, to indulge in a bit of self-forgiveness. That's because the need to forgive ourselves is so doggoned daily and so annoyingly long-term. I speak here with authority and from a great deal of personal experience. For people like me, learning to forgive ourselves is a lifelong lesson, one that I seriously doubt I'll master during my own lifetime. Forgive you? No problem! Forgive myself? Big problem!

The obstacles to self-forgiveness go by many names. Perfectionism. Shame. Guilt. Failure. Blame. Weakness. Regret. Add your own words to the list. What they all add up to is the word *human*. We have a hard time accepting our own humanness. We think we should be above making the mistakes we've made throughout our lives, but we have this head full of negative memories that keep surfacing to make sure we never forget that we're not above it after all. The same brain that cannot recall what I had for dinner last night is the very brain that cannot let me forget the offensive comment I made at the Millville High School Holly Ball in December 1965, a not-so-funny remark that still makes me cringe and brings tears to my eyes when I let it.

So what are we to do about this lifelong dilemma? No one has helped me learn to forgive myself more than author and psychology professor Lewis Smedes. Since I'm still a learner in the self-forgiveness classroom, join me in gaining some insights gleaned from the wisdom of Professor Smedes.

Thankfully for us, Smedes believes the difficulty we have in forgiving ourselves is not such a bad thing. Were it any easier, we'd be inclined to dismiss our serious offenses all too readily. But as difficult as self-forgiveness is, it's also essential to our

Forgive yourself for your faults and your mistakes and move on.

—LES BROWN

sense of wholeness and well-being. Here, the good professor brings logic into play: since it take two to play the blame game, we end up with a divided self—the one doing the blaming, and the one deserving the blame.

"We feel the need to forgive ourselves because the part of us that gets blamed feels split off from the part that does the blaming…. We are exiled from our own selves, which is no way to live," Smedes writes in *The Art of Forgiving*. "This is why we need to forgive ourselves and why it makes sense to do it: We are ripped apart inside, and forgiving ourselves is the only way we heal the split."[5]

Ripped apart inside—that's exactly how we feel when the memories of our bad behavior and the consequences of our bad decisions join forces to condemn us. The image of being the peacemaker who is able to mend the rift between the blaming self and the blamed self is one we would do well to carry with us throughout our lives. Forgiving ourselves becomes an act of self-restoration; we're putting ourselves back together again, making ourselves the whole person we are meant to be.

After imparting this wisdom to us, Professor Smedes doesn't abandon us in the lecture hall; he leads us out into the world where we can apply self-forgiveness principles to our everyday lives. Among his suggestions: Clarify specifically what you need to forgive yourself for. You have the power to grant yourself absolution, so look in a mirror and tell yourself, "God forgives you and so do I"—the sentiment Catholic priests express when granting absolution during confession. Act like a forgiven person acts. Do something impulsive, extravagant, for

The art of being yourself at your best is the art of unfolding your personality into the man you want to be. Be gentle with yourself, learn to love yourself, to forgive yourself, for only as we have the right attitude toward ourselves can we have the right attitude toward others.

—WILFRED PETERSON

another person; "Do anything nice that the practical part of you will tell you is nutty," he writes. "Celebrate the miracle you are performing on yourself by creating a little miracle for somebody else."[6]

Perhaps the most important suggestion of all is to keep granting yourself absolution day after day after day, any time and every time those negative memories crop up. As with forgiving others, it becomes easier to forgive ourselves the more we do it—so those recurring memories may in fact serve a positive purpose in our lives.

Finally, it helps to remember this: if God has forgiven us, who are we to veto his ruling? To do so is tantamount to usurping God's authority and power in our lives—which gives us yet another misdeed to forgive ourselves for. Better to agree with God that we're forgiven and be done with it.

REFLECTION

Self-forgiveness can be an empowering experience, while self-criticism is a particularly draining experience. But maybe you need to be drained of all that self-criticism in order to be filled with power. Close your eyes and criticize all those things you find it so hard to forgive about yourself ... but only under this condition: Imagine God watching you in amusement the entire time. The things we find so hideous about ourselves are usually trifles to God. And all those memories that are so shameful and so embarrassing? You can be fairly certain no one

> Confront the dark parts of yourself, and work to banish them with illumination and forgiveness. Your willingness to wrestle with your demons will cause your angels to sing. Use the pain as fuel, as a reminder of your strength.
>
> —AUGUST WILSON

else remembers them. They're too busy mentally replaying their own shameful and embarrassing moments.

PRACTICE

One of the obstacles to forgiving ourselves is our inability to understand why we have such a hard time with the concept, as well as our unwillingness to take the time to discover precisely what it is that prevents us from forgiving ourselves. You can start to tear down that obstacle right now by completing the following sentence:

I have a difficult time forgiving myself because _____.

Make a list if you have to. You may realize that there are many reasons why you have trouble with self-forgiveness. Some of the most common are the negative messages you may have received as a child, even if you had the best of parents. Nearly all are related in some way to a combination of low self-esteem, a misunderstanding of what forgiveness is, and a misreading of what the Scriptures have to say about forgiveness.

When you're finished with your sentence—or your list—talk it over with God. Imagine a loving God pointing out all the misconceptions you have that are preventing you from forgiving yourself. Then imagine the Spirit leading you into the truth about how and why you should forgive yourself.

> We are not obliged to be perfect once and for all, but only to rise again and again beyond the level of the self. Perfection is divine. All we can do is try to wring our hearts clean in contrition. To be contrite at our failures is holier than to be complacent in perfection.
>
> —ABRAHAM JOSHUA HESCHEL

12 When Death Intrudes

A friend I'll call Janet went through a period when her rage at her husband seemed to know no bounds. After fifteen years of a relatively comfortable marriage, the last five years had been unbelievably frustrating. Bill had washed his hands of any involvement in their family's myriad problems and dumped everything in her lap, expecting her to deal with all of it on her own. More than once, she seriously considered divorcing him. And then, he went and did the worst thing ever: He died, suddenly and without one bit of warning.

Reeling from grief, Janet had no idea how to process her conflicting emotions. She was still mad at Bill for the burden he had placed on her while he was alive, and now she was mad at him for abandoning her so unceremoniously by giving up and dying. Add guilt to the mix, and Janet was one messed up widow. Frankly, I didn't have a clue how to help her at the time. I've since become acutely aware of how inadequately we handle grief in this country; I'm almost beginning to believe that bereavement training should be mandatory. Almost.

Janet needed a way to deal with the resentment that had built up over the years. Since Bill was no longer around to confront, she had to take action in another way. And that way is the way of forgiveness. Only by forgiving him would she be able to let go of her anger and finally be free of the guilt that only added to her burden.

But how do you go about forgiving someone who has died? And how can you ever know that the person accepts your forgiveness? Well, to the second question, the answer is fairly obvious: you can't. Unless … and here's where we get into murky theological territory. Your religious tradition may teach that those who have died are fully aware of what is happening on earth, and your tradition may even encourage you to communicate with the dead. Within Christianity, there's not even complete agreement on the issue; Catholics routinely pray to the dead, while evangelical Protestants consider prayers to the dead to be contrary to God's commands. But one thing is certain—a person who has died is now in a transformed state, a condition that is not bound by the limitations of earthly human life. That, to me, means that those who have gone before us to be with God are the most understanding sorts of beings. I suspect we can have peace in knowing that our forgiveness of someone who has died has accomplished its purpose—if only in our own lives.

Back to the first question: How *do* you go about forgiving someone who has died? I'd say that depends largely on the

Even if you are angry or bitter towards someone who has already died, forgiveness is still possible for you. Because forgiveness is an issue of the heart. And as you forgive, you are going to know God's freedom and liberty in your life.

—DOUG EASTERDAY

Since [God's] command to forgive is absolute, the first order of business is to help [a] person to forgive the deceased. Even if the person we need to forgive has passed away, we are required to release her or him from our unforgiveness.

—CHARLES H. KRAFT

intimacy of the relationship, the nature of the offense, and your own personal needs. Some people need to pour everything out in a long letter to the deceased, citing specific offenses and the specific outcomes in the victim's life. Other people may find it helpful to have an "empty chair" conversation with the person who has died (see the Practice section later in this chapter). In my own experience simply knowing that I've forgiven the person has been enough for me, but that might not have been the case if the person who died had been abusive toward me.

No matter what method you use, it's critical that you be specific about what it is that you're forgiving. Often when loved ones—or not-so-loved ones—die, we're not sure why we're so angry at them. After we've spent some time reflecting on our reaction to their death, we may realize that they never actually offended *us* in the first place. All they did was leave us, and that's what we need to forgive them for. But again, it helps to be specific: forgive your father for his three-pack-a-day habit that robbed your children of their grandfather; your cousin for shooting up with dirty needles and spending her last months in an AIDS hospice without friends or family around her; your best friend for failing to buckle up one lousy time and then overcorrecting when she hit an icy patch in the road. (It's fine, by the way, to redirect your anger—to the tobacco companies, the drug culture, the weather. You only have to get rid of your anger at the person.)

Will forgiving the person diminish your grief, your sense of loss? No, but then that's not the point. The point is to take care of any unfinished business between the two of you. That also applies to your need for forgiveness from someone who dies before you have the opportunity to ask him to forgive you. Seeking his forgiveness through a letter or a "conversation" ties up those loose ends that plague you and contribute to the guilt you feel. But how can you know that he has forgiven you? I stand by my belief that transformed beings are understanding beings, and therefore forgiving beings.

In every death, whether sudden or lingering, there are always unresolved issues. It helps to remember that when you start to feel angry yet *again*—even after you've forgiven the deceased. Grieving takes time, but it's a precious time if you allow it to be. It's a time of performing what Lewis Smedes calls "spiritual surgery" on your memory of the deceased, excising that diseased part of her that needed to be forgiven and restoring her to wholeness in your mind. It's also a time of coming to terms with reality, of recognizing what can and can't be resolved—and of generously bestowing forgiveness on someone who can't even ask for it anymore.

REFLECTION

Do something no one likes to do: reflect on your own mortality. Not in any morbid kind of way and not if it makes you dissolve into a puddle of tears, but in a way that is positive and transformative. Imagine God welcoming you into his presence. Imagine the joy of that moment. Imagine all of this in light of forgiveness and reconciliation—being reconciled with those

> God wants us to be merciful with ourselves. And besides, our sorrows are not our own. He takes them on Himself, into His heart.
>
> —GEORGE BERNANOS

> If you are not already dead, forgive. Rancor is heavy, it is worldly; leave it on earth: die light.
>
> —JEAN-PAUL SARTRE

who have gone before, those you've forgiven and been forgiven by. Think carefully about how that will feel. The image that results will make it clear to you if you have truly granted forgiveness to those people who have died—or if you truly believe they have forgiven you.

PRACTICE

Find a private space and place an empty chair in the room. Pretend that the person who has died is sitting there, and begin to have a conversation with her. This is a time to let it all out—whether it's anger at the way she lorded it over you, the love for her that you never professed, the guilt you feel over not making her go to a doctor earlier, the regret that you never took her to Paris. Imagine her response, but remember that death has transformed her into someone with a nature that may be very different from the nature she had on earth. When you're ready, forgive her for her offenses or ask her forgiveness for yours—or both. Then imagine that the tables—or chairs—are turned, that she is alive and you are the one who has gone on to be with God. Focus specifically on the "with God" part. If you were "with God," would you forgive her? Would you accept her forgiveness? Chances are, you would. Believe that she would do the same.

All religions stress the power of forgiveness, and this power is never more deeply felt than when someone is dying. Through forgiving and being forgiven, we purify ourselves of the darkness of what we have done, and prepare ourselves most completely for the journey through death.

—**SOGYAL RINPOCHE**

A Healthy Choice 13

Making the decision to forgive someone, as it turns out, may be better for you than you realize. In fact, it may be better for you than for the person you forgive. Some have even called it a selfish choice. That's because the health and quality-of-life benefits of a forgiving lifestyle are so many and so dramatic that it's in your own best interest to embrace forgiveness as a regular activity.

Several recent studies on forgiveness came up with an alarming list of physical disorders that result when people harbor resentment and refuse to forgive. Here are just some of the health problems associated with prolonged unforgiveness: high blood pressure and cardiovascular disease; anxiety, depression, and other stress-related disorders; lowered immunity; and a more intense degree of pain in patients with chronic pain.

Those are the physical problems that generally take a long time to show up in a person's health profile. If you were wronged yesterday, it's not likely that your immune system will

We achieve inner health only through forgiveness—the forgiveness not only of others but also of ourselves.

—Joshua Loth Liebman

This is certain, that a man that studieth revenge keeps his wounds green, which otherwise would heal and do well.

—Francis Bacon

be a whole lot weaker today. But there's one symptom of unforgiveness that shows up immediately: clenched jaws and tight facial muscles. We've probably all seen that, and hopefully not in a mirror. People who habitually refuse to forgive can look positively *grim.* This is hardly a scientific finding, but I suspect premature aging can be added to the list of physical results of unforgiveness. And as Norman Vincent Peale once pointed out, all that resentment you've managed to store up doesn't hurt the person you resent, but it does eat away at you night and day—hardly a picture of longevity.

The anger, resentment, and grudges we carry around with us have been likened to a hot coal. Stop a moment and consider how appropriate that metaphor is. Who gets burned by the hot coal we're carrying? We do, obviously. The observation that "Holding on to anger is like grasping a hot coal with the intent of throwing it at someone else; you are the one who gets burned" is attributed to Buddha. It's an accurate observation of the damage we do to ourselves when we refuse to let go of our hostility toward others.

But back to our research studies. Lifestyle issues were also found to be associated with unforgiveness, with higher divorce rates (no surprise there!), and greater problems with substance abuse among people who found it impossible to forgive someone. And, oh, they also had more problems with the other relationships in their lives. Well, gee, I would think so.

It's important, I believe, to take these research findings as validation for our forgiving nature rather than as a blanket prescription. It's not as if you can take a resentful person, tell her to be more forgiving for the sake of her own health and well-being, and expect her to suddenly change her begrudging ways. Even though our mind must make a conscious decision to forgive someone, eventually our heart has to get involved as well. And a change of heart involves more than picking up a refill at Walgreens.

It's good to know, though, that all this forgiving may be making us healthier, isn't it? It's also good to keep that thought in mind whenever we feel the slightest hesitation to forgive someone; we may find that forgiving her comes more easily if we remember that extending forgiveness is clearly in our best interest.

REFLECTION

Reflect on your current state of health and well-being. Unless you're actually sidelined by a physical disorder, you may be tempted to dismiss this as an unnecessary exercise, as I once would have. "I'm just fine!" I would have thought, and I would have gone right on to the next section. But I would have been deceiving myself. Don't follow my lead in this case.

Maybe the only problem you can come up with is that you've had trouble sleeping lately. Give serious consideration to *why*; the reason may be something as simple as one too many mocha lattes or as significant as a host of emotions you've been keeping bottled up for too long. The same goes for digestive disorders; sure, you could blame it on those fast-food burritos, but

Holding on to anger, resentment and hurt only gives you tense muscles, a headache and a sore jaw from clenching your teeth. Forgiveness gives you back the laughter and the lightness in your life.

—JOAN LUNDEN

the culprit just may be that ongoing conflict you have with a coworker. Ask the Spirit to bring to mind every physical or emotional problem you've had lately and then give you the wisdom to know what you need to do to deal with them. (I've learned that God has no problem venturing into the mundane areas of our lives; you may receive the wisdom that what you need to do is bypass the espresso cart.)

PRACTICE

Charles Fillmore, cofounder of the Unity movement, offered this advice for "curing every ill": "Sit for half an hour every night and mentally forgive everyone against whom you have any ill will or antipathy."[7] Try it. Okay, I agree—thirty minutes probably worked better in Fillmore's day. Let's start with five minutes instead.

To carry a grudge is like being stung to death by one bee.
—WILLIAM H. WARTON

Forgiveness is the way to true health and happiness.
—GERALD G. JAMPOLSKY

Radical Forgiveness 14

There's just no way of getting around it: our God is a radical God indeed. We can try with all our might to tame the Spirit, turn God into a kindly old Santa Claus, reduce the Almighty's wild and woolly nature to a soft and sympathetic presence in our lives, but it's not going to change who God is. At least not for long.

Just look at the Bible, starting with the Hebrew scriptures. You learn all these nice (or scary!) little stories when you're a child, but then you put away childish things and begin to read the Bible as an adult. And there, right after the story of Daniel (he of the "lion's den" fame) you come smack up against the book of Hosea. You find yourself reading certain sections over again, because you can't believe you read it right the first time.

Did God really tell Hosea to "find a whore and marry her"? And to "make this whore the mother of your children"? That's how *The Message* expresses the second verse of the book. I'd say that's a fairly radical command, coming from the moral judge of the universe and all. And then—get this!—Hosea's wife won't give up her whoring ways, but God tells Hosea to take her back anyway: "Start all over. Love your wife again, love your wife who's in bed with her latest boyfriend, your cheating wife" (Hosea 3:1).

What on earth did Hosea do to deserve this kind of treatment from the God he served? Nothing. Because this whole episode was not about Hosea at all. It was about God's unending love and forgiveness for the cheating, whoring nation of Israel, which was pursuing other gods at the time. God wanted to show Israel, through Hosea's example, what divine, supernatural love looks like. After letting them have it for most of the book, God promises this: "I will love them lavishly. My anger is played out. I will make a fresh start with Israel" (Hosea 14:4–5).

A fresh start, after Israel's openly defiant and repeated infidelity. That's radical forgiveness. And it worked.

Then along came Jesus, relentlessly preaching a message of forgiveness, telling an oppressed people that they should turn the other cheek and forgive seventy times seven times and insist that they make things right with their enemies before they approach God in worship. He never lets up on this message, never gives people an easy out, never offers them a detour around the tough path of forgiveness and reconciliation.

Jesus didn't suddenly drop out of the sky one day as a fully mature prophet; he grew up in Palestine and was well aware of the strife that existed there. Remember, Palestine at the time was an occupied territory governed by Romans who considered the Jews to be little better than the unwashed masses. Injustice

Let the wicked abandon their way of life and the evil their way of thinking. Let them come back to God, who is merciful, come back to our God, who is lavish with forgiveness.

— ISAIAH 55:7

(THE MESSAGE)

characterized the culture. Despite the wrongs his people experienced, Jesus told them to forgive their oppressors, their persecutors, their abusers. In fact, many Jews who expected Jesus to beat the tar out of the Romans lost faith in him as he continued to preach his radical message of forgiveness and reconciliation. Forgive the oppressors? Never!

The thing is, by modeling radical forgiveness toward us, God has shown us by example that it's possible for us to practice it. Sure, he's God and all, but all we have to do is look around us to see that humans are also quite capable of practicing radical forgiveness. From murder victims' families to the victims of rape and pedophilia, people manage to rise to the occasion to forgive, despite circumstances that make us recoil in horror.

Even after thirty years of hearing Corrie ten Boom's widely known story of radical forgiveness, I cannot get enough of it. Hers is about as compelling an account of human forgiveness as you're likely to find anywhere. In the book *The Hiding Place*, which was made into a movie in the 1970s, she tells of how her Christian family was betrayed by a neighbor for harboring Jews during the Nazi occupation of Holland.

The family was separated, with Corrie and her sister Betsie sent to a concentration camp at Ravensbrück, Germany. Corrie writes of the wretched physical conditions at the camp, as well as the abuse and humiliation inflicted by the SS guards—especially those who mocked and leered at the naked women as they entered the delousing center's shower room. Deprived of sufficient food, warmth, and other necessities, Corrie's beloved

Peace comes when there is no cloud between us and God. Peace is the consequence of forgiveness, God's removal of that which obscures His face and so breaks union with Him. The happy sequence culminating in fellowship with God is penitence, pardon, and peace— the first we offer, the second we accept, and the third we inherit.

—CHARLES H. BRENT

sister became seriously ill and eventually died after failing to receive the medical attention she needed.

Years later, following a church service in Munich at which she had just spoken on forgiveness, Corrie came face-to-face with the greatest challenge of her life. After hammering away at the forgiveness message at one church after another throughout Europe and the United States—and convinced that she had forgiven her oppressors—Corrie was approached by a beaming man whom she recognized as one of the repulsive shower-room guards at Ravensbrück.

Suddenly, the horror and grief she had endured came rushing back to her. "How grateful I am for your message, Fräulein!" the former guard said to her. "To think that, as you say, He has washed my sins away!" As Corrie stood there, frozen, refusing to shake his outstretched hand, she was overcome by her own hypocrisy. "Jesus, I cannot forgive him," she silently prayed. "Give me your forgiveness."

And Jesus did. As she describes it, a "current" passed from her shoulder to her arm to her hand and on to the man as she managed to shake his hand. At that moment, she was overwhelmed with love for him. "And so I discovered that it is not on our forgiveness any more than on our goodness that the world's healing hinges, but on [God's]," she writes. "When he tells us to love our enemies, he gives, along with the command, the love itself."

I don't know of a more powerful story of radical forgiveness, but I know of many that come close. And I know of one element they all hold in common, the supernatural power to for-

If everybody adopted a peaceful, loving, generous, noncompet-itive lifestyle, we could have something better than countercul-ture—we could have the Kingdom of God.

—MARVIN HARRIS

give that can only come from God. Radical forgiveness? A sacred act indeed.

REFLECTION

It's a challenge, to be sure, but try to put yourself in Corrie's place in the church in Munich. Place yourself in the scenario and allow yourself to feel what Corrie must have felt. Remember, she is—you are—widely known for preaching a message of forgiveness. How would you have responded to the guard, given the conflict between your reputation and what you know is right, and the hatred that has just resurfaced and threatens to erupt at any moment? Presumably, Corrie mentioned Ravensbrück in her sermon, and the guard may have realized she was detained in that camp at the same time he served there, though we don't know that for sure. In any event, he is overjoyed that God has forgiven him. How significant do you think Corrie's—your—forgiveness would be to him?

PRACTICE

The word *power* has many connotations, some of them negative. That's just as true in the faith communities as it is in the secular arena. Religious leaders who have abused their power by turning it into a force for evil rather than good have committed a terrible injustice and have given spiritual power a bad name. Meditate on the power that God imparts to us and what

> Forgiveness is the key that unlocks the door of resentment and the handcuffs of hate. It is a power that breaks the chains of bitterness and the shackles of selfishness.
>
> —CORRIE TEN BOOM

69

our responsibility is in using it. Identify the ways that power manifests itself in your own life (such as the power to "turn the other cheek," perhaps, or the power to bring hope to despairing people). Be prepared to help those outside the world of faith understand the distinction between the abuse of power by some religious institutions and leaders, and the magnificence of God's power and the Spirit's willingness to share that power with us.

Forgiveness is an act of the will, and the will can function regardless of the temperature of the heart.

—CORRIE TEN BOOM

Remembering How to Forget

15

There's a wonderful story about Clara Barton, the founder of the American Red Cross, and a woman who had once seriously offended her. A friend who was familiar with the situation was aghast at the kindness Barton displayed toward her offender. Had she taken leave of her senses? Didn't she remember what the woman had done to her? Of course she had. As Barton told her friend, "I distinctly remember forgetting that."

That's a great way to interpret the adage "Forgive and forget." But it's only one way, and it definitely does not apply across the board. There are far too many situations in which it would be irresponsible of us to forget the offenses. The Holocaust and 9/11 come immediately to mind, but atrocities of any kind should never be forgotten. Neither should we forget, or expect anyone else to forget, personal crimes and abuses that have robbed so many people of their loved ones, their sense of security, and their peace of mind.

Be the change that you want to see in the world.

　　—MAHATMA GANDHI

Forgetting is something that time takes care of, but forgiveness is an act of volition, and only the sufferer is qualified to make the decision.

　　—SIMON WIESENTHAL

But let's back up a minute and take a look at the concept of forgetting with regard to forgiveness. First, we need to realize that we never really "forget" anything; it's all stored somewhere in our brains, but our access to a particular bit of information or a specific memory may be limited by any number of factors. So we may think we have forgotten all about an incident that troubled us in the past, but the memory of it is still floating around somewhere.

Second, we need to realize that the kind of forgetting Clara Barton described is an intentional decision to not dwell on what was probably a fairly minor offense. She didn't mean that her brain had destroyed the memory of the offense; what she meant was that she had chosen to go on with her life and her relationship with the offender without allowing the memory of the offense to dominate either one. She simply refused to give her mind permission to replay the tape of the incident.

Third, there's a "forgetting" that's closely akin to denial. This is the kind of forgetting that victims of habitual spousal abuse, for instance, are prone to indulge in. The abused mate forgives the abuser and then forgets—or denies—the very real possibility that the abuse will continue. That kind of forgetting is not only counterproductive but also dangerous. We need to remember situations that proved detrimental to our health and well-being in the past so we'll have the skills and sense to avoid similar situations in the future. And we should always remember to flee dangerous circumstances, no matter how forgiving we are. You can forgive all you like, but call the cops first.

Finally, there's a forgetting that is nothing short of shameful and dishonoring. Do we really want to intentionally forget the Holocaust, 9/11, the bloodshed in South Africa, Sudan, Rwanda, Uganda, the Congo, and God knows how many other countries in Africa and beyond? To do so—or even worse, to live in denial that they have happened—is to bring shame on ourselves and dishonor the memory of the millions who have been slaughtered at the hands of madmen, terrorists, and guerrillas.

So we should feel free to forgive and remember—as long as we don't remember by rewinding and replaying those destructive mental videotapes of every hurtful thing that was ever said or done to us. That only prolongs our agony and reinforces our negative emotions. It does no harm to our offender nor does it do anything to heal our hurts.

I like what a man named Carl Bard once said: "Though no one can go back and make a brand-new start, anyone can start from now and make a brand-new ending." One way to do that is by remembering how to forget—and when not to.

REFLECTION

What has been your experience with intentional forgetting? Maybe it's always been easy for you to purposely dismiss minor offenses, choosing to ignore a cutting remark made by a relative or overlook a friend's failure to include you in a special event. But perhaps it hasn't been quite as easy to forgive someone who

> To forgive heals the wound, to forget heals the scar.
>
> —ANONYMOUS

> It is not "forgive and forget" as if nothing wrong had ever happened, but "forgive and go forward," building on the mistakes of the past and the energy generated by reconciliation to create a new future.
>
> —CAROLYN OSIEK

has hurt you deeply, because you cannot rid your mind of the memory of the incident. How can you apply the balm of intentional forgetting to the deeper wounds in your life without diminishing their significance?

PRACTICE

Intentionally recall one of the worst offenses that was ever done to you. I say "one of" because I don't want you to think you have to relive a horrific experience for this exercise; choose something that wasn't painfully traumatic. Remember the incident in detail—and then ask God to illuminate the situation for you. By shining the light of truth on the situation, you may be able to see some good in it that you were never able to see before. For most of us, very few of the negative incidents in our lives have been entirely bad. Even though you may have had a falling out with someone, you may be able to see for the first time the lasting positive impact she had on your life. Focus on the good that the light reveals, and intentionally forget that which is just not worth remembering.

In forgiving, people are not being asked to forget. On the contrary, it is important to remember, so that we should not let such atrocities happen again. Forgiveness does not mean condoning what has been done. It means taking what happened seriously ... drawing out the sting in the memory that threatens our entire existence.

—**DESMOND TUTU**

Transformational Forgiveness 16

At least two research groups have unearthed a good news/bad news scenario in recent years in separate studies on Americans' attitudes toward forgiveness. Both studies covered a lot of territory, but the findings related to one area of analysis—God's forgiveness—presented a bewildering dichotomy that caught my attention.

The good news is that a considerable majority of Americans—nearly 75 percent—feel as if God has forgiven them, according to the University of Michigan Institute for Social Research. The bad news is that it hasn't made a whole lot of difference in the way many Americans live their lives. That's according to the Barna Research Group, which found that Boomers in particular snapped up the offer of forgiveness presented in the "ask Jesus into your heart" mentality and went on with their lives as if nothing of real consequence had occurred.

"Very few American Christians have experienced a sense of spiritual brokenness that compelled them to beg God for His

A spiritual conversion which was not also a conversion of life was no conversion at all, but a delusion.... The soul cannot be God's and the life not God's at the same time. The soul cannot be recreated and the life remain unchanged ... Where there is no outward change, it is safe to deny an inward change.

—Roland Allen

mercy and acceptance through the love of Christ," Barna pointed out. "We have a nation of 'Christians' who took the best offer, but relatively few who were so humiliated and hopeless before a holy and omnipotent God that they cried out for undeserved compassion."[8]

Humiliated. Hopeless. Spiritually broken. That was me, a bona fide Boomer, on a warm spring night in 1972 when I begged God for forgiveness. Less than a half hour earlier, I had dismissed God, and all that went with God, as nothing more than wishful thinking. Sitting smack in the middle of a roomful of crazy evangelical Christians, I had dismissed them as well. What on earth did these scrubbed and gleaming Barbies and Kens know about sin? Or life, for that matter? And why on earth had I agreed to come to this meeting anyway? So maybe it was a Friday night, and I was bored and didn't have a date, and it was too early for the bars to be worth hitting, and if I went this one time then I could say that there, I went to one of their meetings and it did nothing for me, and my former drinking buddies-turned-Jesus Freaks would have to quit bugging me about giving my life to God and all.

Except it didn't work out that way. Because the speaker that night—a Harley-riding Bible professor I had dismissed as a fraud—spoke nine words in sequence that I could not dismiss: "God not only forgave your sins; he forgot them." Those words hit me with a force that to this day I can't adequately explain. My mind alternately blurred and reeled and snapped to attention and retreated from conscious thought. The only words I recall thinking were these: "What? What did he just say?"

God could *forget* my sins? *I* couldn't do that! How could the judge of the universe do that? Did that mean I was a harsher judge of my sins than even *God* was?

A half hour later, I was a sobbing mass of repentance, unable to utter a word to God. Within minutes, I experienced the floodwaters of love and forgiveness washing over me. Me! In the midst of all those Barbies! Forgiven, reconciled to God, and as time would tell, transformed.

I did not hit the bars that night.

Some of my friends and relatives decided my newfound faith was just a phase. I'd go back to my old way of life, and this whole God thing would become a distant memory. Some of them, I'm sure, are still waiting for that to happen, after thirty-five years.

It won't, though. Because I'm one of those "very few Americans" who experienced a very real sense of spiritual brokenness, and, I suppose, one of the very few Boomers who realized that something of real consequence had occurred in my life that night.

You know, it's easy to argue against theological ideas and spiritual concepts and biblical principles. It's easy, because we have to use words to state our case, and words—even our own words—can become weapons in the hands of those who dispute our claims. But it's difficult to argue against a genuinely transformed life. When my life changed so dramatically that even to others I seemed to become a new person entirely, it's not because I embraced a set of lofty ideas or concepts or principles; it's because I had a life-changing, transforming encounter with

"I can forgive, but I cannot forget" is only another way of saying "I will not forgive." Forgiveness ought to be like a cancelled note— torn in two, and burned up, so that it never can be shown against one.

—HENRY WARD
BEECHER

God that was only made possible by his gracious offer of forgiveness and reconciliation.

God's forgiveness—the real thing, not some bogus, feel-good idea in your head—is transformational. It changes us. It changes us into the kind of person who can, by the power God has given us, make our own gracious offer of forgiveness and reconciliation to others in return.

REFLECTION

Have you had a life-changing encounter with God that was rooted in forgiveness? Have you ever experienced true spiritual brokenness, humiliation, hopelessness? It's when you come to the end of yourself that you can most clearly see God beckoning you to accept the kind of forgiveness that will truly transform your life.

PRACTICE

Ask someone close to you what evidence of transformation they've witnessed in your life. You may be surprised at the response you get; it's possible that you've been transformed in ways you never thought of. Then again, you may not be very happy with the response you get, but that's all part of the process. For instance, your significant other may tell you that you're nowhere near as manipulative as you used to be, and you realize you've walked right into another offense you'll have to

Do not be conformed to this world, but be transformed by the renewing of your mind, so that you may prove what the will of God is, that which is good and acceptable and perfect.

—ROMANS 12:2 (NAS)

forgive. If you approach this practice with an open mind, though, you'll probably end up feeling a whole lot better about yourself in the long run. Other people can see the most amazing things in us—qualities and character traits that we never would have imagined—and it's best that we don't argue with them when they do. Believe that they're the most wise and astute and insightful people in the world.

But we all, with unveiled face, beholding as in a mirror the glory of the Lord, are being transformed into the same image from glory to glory, just as from the Lord, the Spirit.

—2 CORINTHIANS 3:18 (NAS)

17 True Freedom

To forgive is to set a prisoner free and discover
that the prisoner was you.
—Lewis B. Smedes

That's such a powerful quote that I think it deserves to be set apart on a line all its own. It expresses the truth of genuine freedom so succinctly that I have a good mind to go right out and turn it into a bumper-sticker slogan. Wouldn't that be great—bumper stickers that gently encourage forgiveness? Instead of promoting our favorite slimy candidate, we could use our cars to actually make the world a better place.

My newfound bumper-sticker slogan embodies a principle that we all need to remember: we keep ourselves chained to those things and those people that have caused us pain when we allow them to dominate our thoughts. And trust me, when we withhold forgiveness, our thoughts can become consumed by both the offense and the offender.

I've known countless women who have said they're glad to be free of some lousy husband or lover and then continue to criticize and condemn and complain about the lousy guy for months on end. I feel like shouting, "You've got to be kidding me! You're no more free of him than you were when the scoundrel was living with you!" Next time, I just may.

Unforgiveness is the ultimate "closed" human condition. I visualize unforgiveness as a clenched heart—just like a clenched fist that is holding something so tightly that it's causing pain for the person attached to the fist. Think about that image. If you've ever had a cardiac "event," as I have, you know it's nothing you ever want to experience again. Your actual, physical heart seizes up; it feels clenched. For several minutes, everything, like time and life itself, is suspended. Once your heart kicks back in and returns to normal, you'd do whatever it takes to prevent such a thing from ever happening again. If you're smart, that is.

Imagine your other heart—your spirit—seizing up in a similar way. That's what happens when you withhold forgiveness. It turns in on itself, holding onto the offense with an ever tighter grasp. A portion of your life is in a state of suspension; you've lost your heartbeat, the pulse of life that keeps you functioning normally. That's no way to live; that's a way to die.

Let's go back to the prison metaphor. The thing about prison, in a metaphorical sense, is that you can be imprisoned and not even know it. Two images come immediately to mind, one rooted in fact, one in fiction: Communism and *The Matrix*. Many people who were born into a Communist society had no concept of the freedom they were missing out on until they matured and began to learn about the freedoms that people in other countries took for granted. The people living in the fictional Matrix were equally clueless; it was only when they escaped that they could see the prison they were living in.

When you refuse to forgive someone, you still want something from that person, and even if it is revenge that you want, it *keeps you tied to him forever.*

—HENRY CLOUD AND JOHN TOWNSEND

You cannot shake hands with a clenched fist.

—INDIRA GANDHI

When you hold resentment toward another, you are bound to that person or condition by an emotional link that is stronger than steel. Forgiveness is the only way to dissolve that link and get free.

—CATHERINE PONDER

As long as you don't forgive, who and whatever it is will occupy a rent-free space in your mind.

—ISABELLE HOLLAND

Unforgiveness imprisons you in ways you cannot see until you escape its iron bars. You can read a hundred books about the freedom that forgiveness brings, but until you forgive your offender—or accept God's offer of forgiveness—you cannot fathom the astonishing impact it will have on your life. You look back at what life was like before you experienced the freedom of forgiveness, and you cannot believe you ever lived a life of such miserable confinement.

One thing to bear in mind about prison, though. There will always be those prisoners who cannot cut it on the outside. Career criminals often set themselves up to get caught just so they can go back to prison again, where their lives are controlled and their basic needs are met by someone else. Freedom can be frightening, because it requires a person to become responsible, mature, and accountable for her own actions.

Contrary to unforgiveness, forgiveness is the ultimate "open" human condition. It opens our hearts to God and others. It restores the pulse of our lives, and our heart begins to beat for others once again. It releases us from a dark prison of our own making and leads us out into the light. When we finally forgive, we finally know true freedom.

REFLECTION

Come up with a metaphor of your own that illustrates the restraints of unforgiveness and the freedom of forgiveness. Think in terms of closed and open—perhaps a closed-off room whose door is finally opened, letting in light and fresh air for the first time in years. Think about what that image reveals about you, your past or present experiences with forgiveness, and what changes you need to make in your life in order to experience genuine freedom.

PRACTICE

In the book *When You Can't Say "I Forgive You,"* which she wrote with David Hazard, Grace Ketterman tells of a time in a psychiatry class when the discussion turned to healing the scars of trauma. One student had been wiping the tears from his eyes with a handkerchief. The professor told him to hold the handkerchief tightly in his hand, and after a long pause, told him to let it fall. As the man bent down to pick it up, another student observed that in doing so he was picking up his burdens all over again. The incident served as a fitting illustration of the concept of relinquishment—letting go of our burdens for good and finding freedom in the process.

Relinquishment applies to offenses as well. Write out your grievances against someone who has offended you and resolve to forgive the person. Then ceremoniously throw the paper away or burn it.

Two works of mercy set a man free: forgive and you will be forgiven, and give and you will receive.

—St. Augustine

83

18

Just Like Me

Shocking as it may seem, I once sat in judgment of a perfectly formed, perfectly coiffed, perfectly toothed, perfectly tanned little blonde. I didn't know her or anything at all about her, but she was a Jesus Freak, I wasn't, and that's all I needed to know. I only saw her one time, the night in 1972 when God finally broke through my hostility and showered me with his love.

Earlier in the evening, I had singled out this one girl as the target of my disdain for everything Christian. I even hated her for her name, which I won't disclose but which was perfect—her last name actually included the word "love"! How predictable was that?

Later that night, after I crumbled in the presence of God's love, I overheard the perfect Miss Love talking quietly to a group huddled around her to pray for her. As recently as the previous month, she had been a street prostitute. A trusted uncle had abused her throughout her childhood and early adolescence, and she had turned to prostitution in retaliation. And then, four weeks earlier, she turned to God. The group prayed that she would have the strength to avoid returning to her previous lifestyle.

I immediately left the judgment seat.

I once heard a preacher suggest that we try an experiment. Everyone in the service would bring their burdens up front and place them on the altar. Then we'd look over everyone else's burdens and choose which ones we'd like in exchange for ours. He pretty much guaranteed that we'd end up going home with our own burdens; none of us would want the burdens other people carry around on a daily basis.

When we judge other people, when we assume they live perfect lives, when we fail to acknowledge that they just may be experiencing pain of their own, we set up a solid barrier to the free flow of forgiveness from us to those who have hurt us. We disregard the very real possibility that the hurt they have inflicted on us has nothing to do with us at all and everything to do with what is going on in their own lives—or what was going on in their lives decades earlier.

What is it that causes us to forget that other people are also living in pain? We're not the only ones who have negative tapes playing in our heads, reminding us, for example, that we're losers who will never amount to anything. We're not the only ones who have been abused or abandoned or humiliated or whatever.

We look at the person who has offended us—we look at her life, her perfect life—and we cannot believe that there can be

You tend to feel sorrow over the circumstances instead of rage, you tend to feel sorry for the person rather than angry with him.... You understand the suffering that drove the offense to begin with.... It may not have turned out to be a happily ever after, but most certainly there is now a fresh "Once upon a time" waiting for you from this day forward.

—CLARISSA PINKOLA
ESTÉS

any reason, any justification for the way she treated us. Maybe there isn't. But maybe there is. No matter how well you know someone, you cannot know everything that is going on in her life or her head. Let me be blunt here: Even if it's your husband of sixty years, even if it's your closest sibling, even if it's your own child, you do not know it all. We don't know it all about *ourselves*, for heaven's sake.

Admitting that we do not know it all moves us one step closer to forgiveness and reconciliation, because it moves us one step closer to recognizing that other people are just like us. You don't know everything about me. My husband doesn't know everything about me; neither does my sister or my brothers or my daughters. If I offend any of them, they cannot possibly know the myriad and complex factors that provoked the insensitive remark I made. The truth is, *I* don't even know what all those factors are. I want them to cut me some slack; I *need* them to cut me some slack. I'm only human.

And so are those who offend me. They're only human, and I need to cut them some slack. "If we could read the secret history of our enemies," Henry Wadsworth Longfellow once wrote, "we should find in each person's life sorrow and suffering enough to disarm all hostility."[9] By choosing to believe that even the smug and arrogant guy who broke your heart experiences his own sorrow and suffering, you make him human— just like you.

Be kind; everyone you meet is fighting a hard battle.

—JOHN WATSON

REFLECTION

What are the burdens you are carrying? Is your offender aware of the weight on your shoulders? Are you aware of the weight on hers? Do you think your offender would treat you differently if she knew everything that was going on in your life? What does that tell you about how you need to change your attitude toward her?

PRACTICE

Imagine you are God. Some of you won't find that difficult at all. Better yet, imagine that you are a child's version of God, someone "up in heaven" who is looking down at you. Get in character now, because this exercise is about to get rocky. You are God, and you know everything a person is thinking and doing. You are God, and now you are looking down at ... the person who has offended you in your real, I'm-not-actually-God life. What is the offender saying to God about the situation you're embroiled in? What's going on in your offender's life that only God sees? No fair imagining all manner of dastardly deeds that you know the person would never commit; keep it real. Then ask God to give you a compassion for your offender that knows no bounds, now that you realize he is just like you—the I'm-not-actually-God you.

You have to be true to yourself, but you have to be true to your best self, not to the self that secretly thinks you are better than other people.

—STEPHEN GASKIN

19

Growing Up

Remember what life was like when you were fourteen? You couldn't wait to be fifteen, so you could get your permit, or sixteen, so you could get your license. Soon you'd be eighteen, when the state considered you a full-fledged adult. At twenty-one, you could drink—legally. At twenty-five you could even rent a car, though that's generally not high on your list of goals at fourteen. Still, you looked ahead to these milestones and wished you could grow up much, much faster.

Once we reach each of those milestones, we add another notch on the road to maturity. But once we reach whatever magic age we associate with maturity—and especially after we have long passed that age—we realize that maturity has nothing to do with age and everything to do with the way we live our lives.

Growth takes time, but the time it takes varies with each individual. That's true whether the growth is physical, emotional, mental, or spiritual. Spiritual growth is one area that we have a considerable amount of control over. And one of the most valid indications of our spiritual maturity is our willingness and ability to—you guessed it—forgive.

Charles F. Stanley, who as a divorced Baptist pastor knows a bit about forgiving and being forgiven, calls forgiveness the "key to every aspect of spiritual growth."[10] I can't disagree with him. Our response to the difficulties and challenges in life determines the measure of our growth, and those difficulties and challenges nearly always involve the need to forgive someone. Finances, health, and relationships are the key areas in which major problems tend to disrupt our lives, blindsiding us and distracting us with the determination to find someone to blame—which is only natural, so no one should blame us for that.

Our problems worsen, though, the longer we're stuck in the blame rut. Continuing to verbally blame the responsible party, or continuing to seek out someone to blame when the party responsible for our problems isn't all that obvious—that gets us nowhere, but that doesn't stop us from indulging in such a useless activity from time to time. And there is an element to blame that is valid; after all, if there was no one to blame, there'd be no one to forgive. But if all you do is blame—if you finger the perpetrator of the crime but never bring him to trial—you've forfeited the opportunity to further your own spiritual growth by moving from blame to forgiveness. It shouldn't take a whole lot of thought to realize that blame is a characteristic of immaturity; if you need proof, just ask two kids which one of them broke the vase in the living room.

We find comfort among those who agree with us, growth among those who don't.

—FRANK A. CLARK

Forgiveness, by contrast, gets us where we need to be, which is back on the pathway to spiritual growth. It may take a little more thought to realize that forgiveness is a sign of maturity, but consider the characteristics that accompany forgiveness—courage, humility, love, wisdom, trust, responsibility. Not exactly traits you associate with children.

If you want to grow spiritually—if you want to touch the very heart of God and align your spirit with God's Spirit—you have to let go of every last shred of unforgiveness in your life. Spiritual maturity demands that. To be aligned with God's Spirit is to respond in a godly—mature—way to those responsible for the difficulties you face. And that requires forgiving them, because where God is, there is always forgiveness.

REFLECTION

What does maturity mean to you? Do you consider yourself mature? Meditate on the concept of spiritual maturity, expecting God's Spirit to reveal to you those areas of your life where you've grown significantly and those areas where you could use some help. Ask for the grace to accept the difficult situations that will ultimately help you grow.

PRACTICE

Look at your life in terms of your spiritual growth. Many people want to be spiritually mature, but they do precious little

> The human family is our best illustration of how each person grows in his unique potentialities by sharing in the loving care of a society of other persons. Yet each member of the family discovers what it is to give of himself for the sake of the others.
>
> —DANIEL DAY WILLIAMS

> When we see problems as opportunities for growth, we tap a source of knowledge within ourselves which carries us through.
>
> —MARSHA SINETAR

to foster growth in their spiritual lives. Knowledge and experience are two of the key elements of spiritual growth. By learning about God and our faith tradition through books, sermons, and the like, we grow in knowledge; by stepping out in faith, taking risks, and serving others, we grow in experience.

The problem is, some of us gravitate toward one type of growth to the exclusion of the other. If you're spiritually knowledgeable but lacking in down-to-earth experience, do something outside your comfort zone that will broaden your horizon of faith. If you have all the experience in the world but little formal learning, expand your knowledge by enrolling in a religion course or choosing a faith-related book to read.

You always grow in difficult times. Your life may change, it may never be the same, but you learn more about yourself than at any other time in your life.

—PICABO STREET

Anger makes you smaller, while forgiveness forces you to grow beyond what you were.

—CHERIE CARTER-SCOTT

20 Lasting Peace

Thomas Takashi Tanemori was just about the last person on earth you would have expected to extend forgiveness to the people he hated the most—Americans.

For forty years, Tanemori harbored bitterness and anger toward America, and with good reason. Tanemori was a young child living in Hiroshima, Japan, in 1945 when the United States dropped an atomic bomb on the city, killing his parents, two sisters, his grandparents, and nearly all his friends. Radiation from the blast eventually robbed him of his eyesight. He has since survived a bout with stomach cancer, as well as several heart attacks. He once attempted suicide.

Today, though, Tanemori lives in the country he hated and has forgiven the people he blamed for the overwhelming loss he suffered. He found lasting peace in 1985, when he was finally able to forgive America and its citizens—partly as a result of recalling his father's words: "Respect all who are living."

Now a Baptist pastor, Tanemori is founder of the Silkworm Peace Institute in California, which isn't your typical organization dedicated to peace. Rather than focusing on peace as the absence of war, Tanemori promotes the kind of peace that comes when the heart is transformed by God. He considers extending love and forgiveness to be the best alternative to revenge.

Few of us can comprehend the magnitude of Tanemori's loss, but we may be able to relate to the desire for vengeance that once consumed him. He lived in turmoil for four long decades, wanting to see his enemies suffer for what they had taken from him. Too many of us have lived our lives in a similar state of turmoil, and with far less justification. Our unforgiveness toward others has robbed us of the inner peace that God has assured us we could have in this lifetime. We carry around the burden of past offenses that weigh us down and grow heavier as we add more offenses to the pile.

What is wrong with us, anyway?

I'm going to take a stab at answering that and suggest that we really don't believe inner peace is attainable, and certainly not by doing something nice for our enemies such as forgiving them. Then along comes a Hiroshima survivor who says, yes, it really is attainable, and yes, you find inner peace through forgiveness. He's someone worth listening to, don't you think?

There are some people, though, who won't listen to him or to you or to me, because they've allowed the turmoil to grow so intense that they *can't* listen. I'm sure you know someone like that; they're the "Yes, but" people in our lives, the ones who

> To forgive is the highest, most beautiful form of love. In return, you will receive untold peace and happiness.
>
> —ROBERT MULLER

> We should have much peace if we would not busy ourselves with the sayings and doings of others.
>
> —THOMAS À KEMPIS

simply can't find their way through the thicket of their problems even though the solution may be just on the other side. It's mentally and emotionally draining to even try to be a friend to someone like that; about the best you can do is to try to *be* the peace that keeps eluding them.

But back to the rest of us. Maybe we're just skeptical about this whole inner peace thing. We're willing to listen, but we remain unconvinced. There's only one way we can be convinced, and that's by actually laying our burdens down and getting rid of them for good when we finally, *finally*, take that leap of faith and forgive our offenders.

The peace that comes through forgiveness is the kind of peace that lasts. And it can wipe away years—decades, even—of turmoil in one moment of grace.

God's peace is joy resting. His joy is peace dancing.

—F. F. BRUCE

REFLECTION

Think about your life in terms of peace—genuine, inner peace. Can you say you are at peace—with God, with others, with yourself? If not, what can you do to acquire it? How can you turn down the noise so you can hear what God wants to do to restore peace to your life?

PRACTICE

Pray this prayer from Søren Kierkegaard in your personal prayer time:

To thee, O God, we turn for peace; but grant us, too, the blessed assurance that nothing shall deprive us of that peace, neither ourselves, nor our foolish, earthly desires, nor my wild longings, nor the anxious cravings of my heart.

Pax Christi, a Catholic peace movement, offers this prayer for peace and reconciliation for liturgical use:

We confess that in our lives we do not always choose the way of peace. We spread gossip which fans the flame of hatred. We are ready to make any sacrifices when Caesar demands—but few when God invites. We worship the false god of security and nationalism. We hold out our hand in friendship—but keep a weapon in the other behind our back. We have divided your body of people into those we trust and those we do not. Huge problems challenge us in the world—but our greed, fear and selfishness prevent us from uniting to solve them.

Lord, we pray for your help, your forgiveness and your reconciling power in our lives.

There is no peace without forgiveness. Attack thoughts towards others are attack thoughts towards ourselves.

—MARIANNE WILLIAMSON

Forgiving those who hurt us is the key to personal peace.

—G. WEATHERLY

Inner peace can be reached only when we practice forgiveness. Forgiveness is letting go of the past, and is therefore the means for correcting our misperceptions.

—GERALD JAMPOLSKY

21
Overlooking the Trivial

With all this emphasis on forgiveness, you could easily get the impression that I believe we need to forgive each and every thing that's done to us. Likewise, you may get the impression that I believe we need to ask forgiveness for each and every thing we do. Just the opposite is true; I consider forgiveness so valuable that I believe it should be extended and sought only in those situations that are equal to it in importance.

Look, if you feel you need to ask for your friend's forgiveness for taking the last piece of chocolate from the Godiva box, I'm not going to stop you. (But only if you share.) And far be it from me to tell you that you shouldn't forgive your husband for hogging the remote; couples have separated over less serious issues than that, I'm sure. The thing is, like anything else, we can carry forgiveness to such an extreme that it can become a burden, a meaningless gesture, or a legalistic obligation.

Let me tell you how it became a legalistic obligation in one church I attended. The leader of the women's group had always struck me as a wise, loving, and down-to-earth person. One night, though, she made the comment that if you died with any unconfessed and therefore unforgiven sin in your life, you'd go straight to hell. Whoa! I don't know what she was thinking; I was so taken aback by what she said that it took a few seconds longer than it should have for me to process her words. A newer and younger member of the group immediately spoke up, out of fear, I'm sure, and asked if that meant she would go to hell if she had a sinful thought but died before she had time to ask God to forgive her. The leader assured her that yes, she would indeed go to hell.

I have to tell you, I really think the leader responded the way she did only because she felt as if she had been backed into a corner. Actually, in my mind I've tried every which way to get her out of this mess and still have respect for her as a wise and loving person. But I can't. I didn't know what to make of her off-the-wall comment then, and I don't know what to make of it now. Except for this: Anytime we set a spiritual principle in stone, we run the risk of turning it into a life-robbing obligation rather than the spirit-freeing guideline that it is.

Does God want us to seek forgiveness when we blow it? Of course. But come on. If God expected us to seek forgiveness for every little thing we did wrong, we wouldn't have time to eat, drink, or, well, live. (And don't even get me started on the hell part of the leader's little teaching. There aren't enough hours in the day....) God expects us to use the sense we were born with and not live our lives in a never-ending process of exacting self-reflection.

> The art of being wise is the art of knowing what to overlook.
>
> —WILLIAM JAMES

> See everything, overlook a great deal, correct a little.
>
> —POPE JOHN XXIII

So maybe we've mastered the fine art of overlooking our own little foibles. But what about the foibles of other people? What about the author who made you share that last piece of Godiva chocolate with her? Don't you need to forgive her? And how about that weasel at work who always takes the last drop of coffee but never makes a fresh pot? Or the letter carrier who is always and forever putting the wrong mail in your box, which sends you into a tailspin of worry over who your mail is being delivered to and what they've done with the Publishers Clearing House letter confirming that you really did in fact win the million-dollar sweepstakes, and that thought forced you to stay up all night in despair over how they're going to know that you are the only valid winner and now you just sit by the window all day wringing your hands as you wait for the Prize Patrol to drive up?

Some things we're better off overlooking.

Learn to overlook the trivial stuff—the minor irritations and annoyances that are part and parcel of everyday life. We'll never be rid of them; we might as well get used to them, do what we can to change the irritating situations—tell the author to back off, ask the weasel to make a pot of coffee, talk to the letter carrier *again*—and shrug it all off as the comparatively minor stuff that it is. Save your gift of forgiveness for the major offenses. They're almost certain to come.

Our souls may lose their peace and even disturb other people's, if we are always criticizing trivial actions—which often are not real defects at all, but we construe them wrongly through our ignorance of their motives.

—St. Teresa of Ávila

REFLECTION

Are you majoring on the minors—allowing the little things to become far more important than they should? Lots of people do this without realizing it. In fact, you could have a good laugh over someone's else's "mountain out of a molehill" experience one minute and make your own mountain the next, oblivious to the irony of what you've just done. Examine your life for evidence of little things that have unnecessarily grown to become big things.

PRACTICE

Go through your day determined to overlook trivial offenses and problems. At the end of the day, evaluate how you did, and allow yourself to chuckle over the many times you were tempted to make something out to be more important than it was. Do the same the next day. Did you fare any better?

What ever the motive for the insult, it is always best to overlook it; for folly doesn't deserve resentment, and malice is punished by neglect.

—SAMUEL JOHNSON

Depression is nourished by a lifetime of ungrieved and unforgiven hurts.

—PENELOPE SWEET

22 Forgiveness Is Not Reconciliation

One of the greatest impediments to forgiving others is the mistaken belief that forgiveness equals reconciliation. It does not. Forgiveness is something we all have the power to grant to another person, but none of us has the power to force reconciliation on someone who does not want it. And sometimes, the person who does not want reconciliation is the person we see in the mirror every morning. Some of the very people who willingly grant forgiveness are unwilling to restore a relationship with their offender, and with good reason.

Joyce Meyer, an evangelist and bestselling author, has spoken and written extensively about the sexual, emotional, physical, and verbal abuse her father inflicted on her until she left home at the age of eighteen. Her situation was truly horrendous, and how she came to see God as a loving Father—which is who she perceives God to be—is nothing short of miraculous given the image of fatherhood she carried with her throughout her life.

Meyer also writes and speaks a lot about forgiveness and reconciliation, and when she does, people pay attention. She tells how she spent much of her adult life in private misery, despite what she thought was a good relationship with God, an active church life, and a wonderful family life. Little did she realize that the bitterness she harbored against her father and others who had abused her decades earlier was the cause of her despair. She had never dealt with the abuse she suffered, and its aftereffects were eating away at her.

Once she realized what was going on, it still took a considerable amount of prayer, time, and grace before Meyer was able to let go of the bitterness and anger that was ruining her life, which gave her the freedom to finally forgive her father. Eventually, she even attempted to reconcile with her father. But she was ill-prepared for his response. Her father denied that he had done anything wrong. To make matters worse, he blamed Meyer for causing the problems between them.

There was no way she could resume a relationship with him. Until he owned up to the damage he had done—and until he stopped accusing her—Meyer's father was hardly a candidate for reconciliation.

Like Meyer, millions of women—and men—have suffered multiple types of abuse at the hands of people in their lives that they should have been able to trust. Forgiving an abuser is difficult enough; attempting to rebuild a relationship with an abuser is something you need to think long and hard about first. Sometimes, reconciliation is simply unwise; other times, it's downright dangerous.

> Reconciliation is not the same as forgiveness, and letting someone who hurt you back into your life is not the same as truly letting go of the pain.
>
> —SIDNEY B. SIMON

101

Many people ... think that in order to forgive, they must enter back into an active relationship with the person who has injured them. That is not true, and this misconception has caused a problem for many people who want to forgive.

—JOYCE MEYER

Anyone who tries to make you believe that forgiveness always requires reunion is someone who neither understands forgiveness nor has your best interests at heart. And that includes religious leaders. Many Christian women in particular feel pressured to return to their abusers if their church delivers a strong message against divorce. If a woman has forgiven her husband, the leaders reason, she should be willing to reconcile with him—even if the abuse continues. I've actually heard that preached, but thankfully, not in a long, long time.

There's another reason, though, why Christian women feel they need to make every effort to reconcile with their offenders, and that's the teachings of the New Testament. We are encouraged to live in harmony with each other and to be reconciled to each other. It's clear that God wants us to be at peace with others, but frankly, I'm not so sure that means we need to be in relationship with those "others." Living with an abuser is hardly the same as living in peace with him.

Meyer, by the way, was eventually reconciled to her father, but only after he genuinely repented of the suffering he inflicted on her in so many ways and for so many years. Without that, and until he had proven that he could be trusted not to hurt her again, reconciliation was not a possibility. Empty promises don't count; only a transformed life, one that has proven its trustworthiness over time, is a candidate for true reunion.

REFLECTION

Imagine the relationship you would like to have with someone you have forgiven but have yet to be reconciled with. Be realistic. Consider what your relationship was before, the nature of the offense, and the level of trust you have in the person right now—not that wishful-thinking level of trust you hope to have in the future. If the offender was once your closest friend and confidant, you may need to ratchet down your expectations considerably, settling for an occasional lunch date instead of the daily heart-to-heart conversations you had grown accustomed to. If the offender was a serious abuser, your best description of the relationship you would like to have may very well include the word "non-existent." Just be honest with yourself, and then you'll have a clear idea of what you need to work toward in order to rebuild the relationship.

PRACTICE

Pray this prayer for reconciliation:

> Lord, I have forgiven my abuser. If reconciliation is to be a result, I trust you to give me the grace to do whatever it takes to restore the relationship. If reconciliation is not a wise course to take, help me to be at peace with that decision. And if I have lingering bitterness toward my offender that is blocking a

We can forgive even if we do not trust the person who wronged us once not to wrong us again. Reunion can happen only if we can trust the person who wronged us once not to wrong us again.

—**LEWIS B. SMEDES**

reconciliation that you desire, I ask that you would soften my heart and enable me to extend genuine and complete forgiveness to my abuser. Give me the wisdom I need to protect myself and live in peace with others. Amen.

We must make our homes centers of compassion and forgive endlessly.

—MOTHER TERESA

Choosing to Reconcile 23

Now that you understand the distinction between forgiveness and reconciliation, it may be time to determine whether you would like to be reconciled with your offender. Unlike forgiveness, which can happen in an instant, reconciliation can be a lengthy process, starting with the decision to pursue reconciliation right through to the time when trust has been restored.

The first thing we all need to remember is that the decision to reconcile is ours and ours alone. No one can make you pursue reconciliation with your offender, and no one can force you to reconcile with someone who is seeking a renewed relationship with you. Don't let anyone make you feel guilty about your reluctance to reconcile; reconciliation is not a condition of forgiveness. If you have forgiven someone, that can be the end of it if you want it to be.

The second thing to remember is that just because you have begun to consider the prospect of reconciliation, it doesn't mean you have to follow through with it. What seems like a good

God works within the tragic destiny of human efforts with a healing power, and a reconciling spirit. Even those who have felt completely superior to all "outworn" religious notions must look today at least wistfully to the possibility that such a God lives and works.

—D. D. WILLIAMS

idea now could turn out to be a bad idea later on, after a great deal of soul-searching, prayer, and counsel with people whose judgment you value.

The third thing to remember is that you have no control over the outcome. Your offender may not be the slightest bit interested in resuming a relationship with you, and that's all right. You made your move, you did your best, and now it's out of your hands. It may turn out that a failed attempt at reconciliation is the best thing that ever happened to you.

Let's say you've passed through the soul-searching, prayer, and counseling phase, and you've decided that yes, you would like to try to restore your relationship with a friend who betrayed you. She has expressed remorse, sought your forgiveness, and received it. Still, you feel estranged from her. What now?

It's important that you carefully consider how to approach your friend—should you call, e-mail, visit? I remember something Bill Gothard said during his Institute in Basic Youth Conflicts seminar, which was popular in churches in the 1970s and 1980s. He discouraged people from seeking forgiveness and reconciliation in writing. "You want to erase the offense," he said, "not document it."[11]

Once you've decided how you'll approach your friend, it's wise to let that decision rest for a while. Your forgiveness can be immediate, but you shouldn't feel rushed into a reconciliation. You want to do it the right way, taking your need for emotional protection and respect for your friend's needs into consideration. If it seems she's been avoiding you, it may be because she's still ashamed of her behavior even though you've forgiven her. But it could also be that the incident made her realize that it's best for the two of you to remain cordial acquaintances instead of best buddies. You'll need to provide an out for her, a way to allow her to decline your offer of reconciliation and still save face. That may seem unfair to you, but if the relationship is so important to you that you want to reconcile, you need to be prepared to do some hard things. Attempts at reconciliation are both risky and challenging.

In any event, if your offender wants to be reconciled, you still need to proceed with caution. Restoring trust takes a great deal of time and requires a noticeable change in behavior on the offender's part. If your offender rejects your initial attempt at reconciliation but you still have hope for a relationship in the future, you need to proceed with extreme caution. Maybe you're right; maybe the two of you belong together, and the person who offended you just needs more time work everything out in his own mind and realize that the two of you should get back together. But maybe you're wrong; your hope for a future relationship is just wishful thinking. You need to have all your senses finely honed to determine what the truth is about your situation. And always remember this—if the past relationship involved abuse, you need to proceed with extreme caution, the advice of a counselor, and possibly the assistance of a mediator.

Have I convinced you that this is a decision not to be taken lightly? I hope so. Remember this: It's far better to experience a failed attempt at reconciliation than a failed reconciliation

Sincere forgiveness isn't colored with expectations that the other person apologize or change. Don't worry whether or not they finally understand you. Love them and release them. Life feeds back truth to people in its own way and time.

—SARA PADDISON

Keep on loving your friends; do your work in welcoming hearts.

—PSALM 36:10
(THE MESSAGE)

itself. The first offers the comfort of knowing you did what you believed was right, even if it didn't work out; you can get on with your life with a clear conscience. The latter reopens old wounds, compounding the initial hurt you experienced; moving forward after a failed reconciliation is especially difficult. Take it slow, and take it carefully. Take it to your counselors, and take it to God. You'll need all the support you can get.

REFLECTION

Think about what you have to gain in reconciling with someone. Think also about what you have to lose. Weigh the outcomes of each approach, reconciling or not reconciling. Can you realistically get on with your life if you choose not to reconcile?

PRACTICE

Once you've made the decision to reconcile, it's rehearsal time. Mentally play out the ideal reconciliation scene. Imagine the conversation you would like to have with your friend—what you will say first, what she will say in return. You're the writer, director, and one of the actors, so you have a lot of control over this exercise. Try out different scenarios, different ways of approaching your friend, and different responses from your friend. Prepare for a variety of outcomes. When the time comes to have the real-live reconciliation scene, you'll be in a better position to handle whatever transpires.

Many promising reconciliations have broken down because while both parties came prepared to forgive, neither party came prepared to be forgiven.

—CHARLES WILLIAMS

Friends come and friends go, but a true friend sticks by you like family.

—PROVERBS 18:24

(THE MESSAGE)

24
Setting Boundaries

Mark and Cathy—not their real names—were long-ago acquaintances of mine from a church in New Jersey. At the time that I knew them, I was between marriages and prone to find a happy couple at every turn. Some of you know what I mean. When you're alone and miserable, all the world's a couple—a deliriously, blissfully ecstatic couple. You, on the other hand, seem to be the only unattached person left on the planet.

Cathy and I probably could have been good friends, except for the fact that there she was happily married and all. It was hard seeing her husband lavish so much affection on her, so I kept my distance. He wasn't sappy or anything; he just appeared to be genuinely in love with her, even after nine years and three children. After we all went out for pizza one night, I rode home with Lynn, Cathy's closest friend. "Mark is one of the good guys," I said. "I can tell."

Right.

A year or so later, after I learned that Mark had been unfaithful to Cathy pretty much since their honeymoon, I remembered Lynn's silence in response to my astute observation. When Mark and Cathy separated and later divorced, I immediately joined the chorus of critics who denounced Mark's despicable behavior every time we talked to Cathy. We were in her corner, cheering her on to a better, Mark-free life.

Problem was, inexplicably and unknown to us, Cathy still loved Mark. And in spite of himself, Mark still loved Cathy. Since they weren't exactly on good terms or even speaking terms—she had moved out of state and taken the kids with her—neither one knew how the other felt.

Mark's guilt nearly crushed him, but before the damage was complete, he broke down and got into some committed therapy for a serious amount of time. Meanwhile, Cathy began to see a counselor in her new church, which proved to be a much safer place to confess her love for Mark than among her Mark-hating friends. With his therapist's blessing, Mark drove a thousand miles to tell Cathy how sorry he was and to ask her if she thought she might someday be willing to consider the possibility of forgiving him. He decided that the best he could hope for was that she would not shoot him, which he felt she had every right to do.

Cathy didn't shoot him. To Mark's surprise, she forgave him. He had no way of knowing that for nearly a year she had been working toward forgiving him. He was so shocked, in fact, that he blurted out a question he'd never had any hope of asking: "Does that mean you think we can get back together?"

Forgive, but guard your heart until you see sustained change.

—HENRY CLOUD AND
JOHN TOWNSEND

Now, Cathy still loved the man, but she wasn't what you'd call stupid. Her incredulous look was all the answer Mark needed. After spending some much-needed time with the children, Mark returned to New Jersey, figuring it was all over once again.

Back in her counselor's office, Cathy identified the behaviors—aside from the obvious one—that had troubled her about Mark all along, actions that she now realized should have tipped her off to her husband's affairs. With her counselor's help, she created a list of non-negotiable conditions that Mark would have to fulfill before she would consider reconciliation. Her list started out like this:

1. Continue seeing his therapist. Cathy credited him with challenging Mark to take a hard look at himself and make difficult but necessary changes.

2. Exhibit faithfulness and responsibility in other areas of his life—toward God, toward his employer, toward his biological family, toward his children.

3. Find an accountability partner, a man who would make a commitment to meet with Mark weekly to help him maintain his integrity through open and honest dialogue.

In all, the list included seven conditions. By defining what she expected of Mark, Cathy established the boundaries that would protect her as they took their first small steps toward rebuilding a relationship. Mark's willingness to abide by her

Forgiveness is the most tender part of love.

—JOHN SHEFFIELD

111

wishes helped restore her trust in him. Only after Mark had proven himself over an extended period of time did Cathy even consider a full reconciliation.

Four years after their divorce, Mark and Cathy remarried. Mark agreed to a new set of requirements that applied to their married life ... and Cathy did the same. Over the years, she had examined the behaviors of her own that had contributed to the failure of their first marriage. Mark and her counselor collaborated on a list of conditions Cathy would have to meet. Both Mark's list and Cathy's included this item: participate in regular marriage counseling sessions.

The last I heard, Mark and Cathy had celebrated twenty-three years of marriage, give or take that four-year break.

Establishing clear, measurable, and realistic boundaries is a sound practice for all of us to follow. It's especially important for anyone seeking the restoration of a relationship that was broken by infidelity or abuse or a similar serious offense. Just as important is maintaining the boundaries you have set. If you agree to reconcile with your abusive father on the condition that your only contact is by phone, for example, then you need to be prepared to stand your ground if he shows up at your door, playing on your sympathy in the hope that your good nature will win out over your resolve.

This is one of the greatest obstacles to releasing women from the control of the abusive men in their lives. Some women either fail to draw clear boundaries that define what they absolutely will not tolerate in a relationship, or they manage to forget those boundaries when their abusers show up with

> Forgiveness is not the misguided act of condoning irresponsible, hurtful behavior. Nor is it a superficial turning of the other cheek that leaves us feeling victimized and martyred. Rather it is the finishing of old business that allows us to experience the present free of contamination from the past.
>
> —JOAN BORYSENKO

empty promises and an uncanny ability to convince them that things will be different this time. It's all well and good to forgive your abuser, but make it clear that you have regained control of the situation by drawing a huge and unmistakable line that he is never to cross.

It's a mistake to think of boundaries in a negative way, as if they were the walls of a prison. They're not. They're more like the walls of a fortress. They are not meant to restrict you but to protect you. When it comes to you and your emotional—and perhaps physical—well-being, living within boundaries gives you control over not only who may enter your life but also the conditions under which they may do so. You may permit entrance to someone who once hurt you, but he must leave his weapons behind.

REFLECTION

Visualize your life as a fortress designed to protect you and not to isolate you. There will be times in your life when the drawbridge is down, when your welcoming and generous spirit allows others to enter freely. At other times—especially after you've been hurt—the drawbridge will be up, the gates closed, the doors padlocked. What will it take for you to allow someone—anyone—into your fortress under those circumstances?

Keep vigilant watch over your heart; that's where life starts.

—**PROVERBS 4:23**

(THE MESSAGE)

PRACTICE

No matter what your present situation is, it's a good idea to get clear about what your boundaries are in all relationship categories—friendship, romance, work-related, family, and so on. You won't be able to cover every possibility, because you often don't know what your limitations are until someone comes right up against them—or violates them. But you can have a pretty good idea what you will and will not tolerate, based on your previous experiences. Say you work in an environment where your coworkers routinely trade favors—you flip the burgers for me when I'm overloaded, and I'll cut the tomatoes for you when you're overloaded. But then there's Sam, who never, ever gets those sesame seed buns toasted without imposing on you and me, which puts us on overload when we return to our own work. The line you draw will be right at the point where Sam's inability to do his own work begins to affect yours. Write down everything that comes to mind as you're doing this exercise. Later on you can delete those things that either don't really bother you all that much or that seem excessive compared to everything else on your list. The main point is to clarify what your boundaries are—for yourself right now, and for others later on.

Without forgiveness life is governed by an endless cycle of resentment and retaliation.

—ROBERTO ASSAGIOLI

Listening with Your Heart 25

Vietnamese monk Thich Nhat Hanh is a prominent Buddhist author whose books have attracted the attention of people of all faiths, and with good reason. He became prominent not by drawing attention to himself but by the wisdom of his teachings and the example of his life. One of the practices he has incorporated into the daily routine of his monastery in France is a simple but profound one used by the monks who answer the telephone: before they pick up the handset, they take one deep breath to disconnect from whatever they are doing and a second deep breath to connect with the caller. This practice prepares them to give the caller their full attention.

I'm afraid this is one exercise in mindfulness—or being fully present in the moment—that I fail at time and again. I am decidedly not a telephone person. Oh, I'll give the telephone credit for making it easy to schedule appointments and such, but once a call reaches the five-minute mark, I start to get antsy. Really antsy. Heaven help the caller if I'm at the computer; I often keep right on working, striking the keys as quietly as possible and making sure the speakers are turned off.

Fully present in the moment? Hardly. Mindful? Of my work maybe, but not of the caller.

Thich Nhat Hanh's phone-answering practice hasn't changed mine, but it has impacted my life in another way. It's made me aware of how seldom I disconnect from whatever I'm doing and give my full attention to someone who is talking to me. Not only is that disrespectful, but also the failure to listen attentively—and without judgment—seriously impedes our efforts at reconciliation.

Whether another person is attempting to reconcile with you or you are the one seeking to reconcile, you owe it to yourself to listen carefully to what is and isn't being said in the conversation at hand. (You also owe it to the other person if only out of respect for his humanity, though you may not accept that notion right now.) By listening carefully—that is, not just with your ears but with your heart as well—you may discover that it was a misunderstanding that caused you to part ways in the first place, that you were far more responsible for the rift than you ever thought—or that reconciliation in this particular case is not a wise move after all.

Listening with the heart requires a genuine desire to understand what the other person is saying. It also requires a set of practical listening skills that we all would do well to master. Kay Lindahl, founder of The Listening Center and author of *The Sacred Art of Listening*: *Forty Reflections for Cultivating a Spiritual Practice* (SkyLight Paths), has developed nine general

You must understand this, my beloved: let everyone be quick to listen, slow to speak, slow to anger.

—JAMES 1:19 (NRSV)

guidelines for "deep listening"; after each one of her guidelines I've shown how it applies to efforts at reconciliation:

One. Suspend assumptions. Don't interpret the other person's meaning according to your own experience. Recognize that she is speaking out of her own circumstances, which differ from yours—perhaps greatly.

Two. Use "I" language. When it's your turn to speak, avoid using the word "you," which can sound unnecessarily confrontational and accusatory.

Three. Listen without judgment. This one is tough for many people, but do your level best to resist the urge to think in terms of right or wrong, good or bad, true or false as the other person is speaking.

Four. Suspend status. This is where parents often derail attempts at reconciliation with their children. Treat the other person as someone who is on equal footing with you. This is no time to pull rank.

Five. Maintain confidentiality. The very act of seeking forgiveness or reconciliation is humbling enough; don't add humiliation to the mix by revealing to others the sordid details that you know should be kept private.

Six. Listen for understanding. Another tough one. Enter into a reconciliation dialogue with the awareness that you don't have to agree with everything the other person says; you simply have to try to see the situation from his perspective.

Seven. Ask questions. If you don't understand the point the other person is making even after careful listening, ask carefully worded questions to gain clarity.

All who strive for reconciliation seek to listen rather than to convince, to understand rather than to impose themselves.

—BROTHER ROGER

Eight. Be silent. You don't have to fill every space with words. At times, you may both need to reflect on what has just been said.

Nine. One at a time. This is a biggie. Do not—*do not*—interrupt the other person, no matter how much you disagree with her, how wrong you think she is, how angry she just made you. Especially if you're angry. Hold your tongue and calm yourself down.

I'll add a tenth guideline, compliments of the great spiritual leader and writer François Fénelon: "Listen less to your own thoughts and more to God's thoughts." That's what it really means to listen with your heart.

Take a deep breath. Disconnect from your own thoughts. Take another deep breath, and let God's thoughts—about you, about the other person, about the entire situation—supersede yours. Be open to the Spirit's leading; be vulnerable to the Spirit's power to transform; be willing to consider the Spirit's creative path to reconciliation.

REFLECTION

Think back to a difficult or uncomfortable conversation you recently experienced. Analyze what went wrong (or right) according to Kay Lindahl's guidelines—and Fénelon's.

> The first duty of love is to listen.
>
> —PAUL TILLICH

PRACTICE

See if you have better success than I did with Thich Nhat Hanh's telephone-answering ritual. Try to get in the habit of taking two deep breaths when the phone rings—one to disconnect from what you're doing, and one to fully connect with the caller.

There is a grace of kind listening, just as there is a grace of kind speaking.

—FREDERICK WILLIAM

FABER

26 Seventy Times Seven

At various times during Jesus's three-year ministry his disciples would come to him with a bunch of questions that they hoped would clarify some of his teachings. They were a fairly dense lot, those disciples; in the Gospel of Mark in particular you get the impression that more than once they even manage to exasperate Jesus. You can just see them losing sleep over a teaching that they can't quite get. In Peter's case, that would be Jesus' teaching on forgiveness, among others. And so he asks this priceless question: "Lord, if another member of the church sins against me, how often should I forgive? As many as seven times?"

Now really. I ask you: What was Peter thinking? Was he trying to quantify forgiveness? Was he hoping Jesus would help him justify his unforgiving spirit by saying that once was enough—after that, the person did not deserve a second chance? Did Peter even hear what he was asking? The question is so absurd that *The Message* paraphrase implies that it took some nerve for Peter to ask it.

Since Peter seemed to pull the number seven out of thin air, Jesus responds on Peter's level by pulling his own number out of thin air—seventy times seven, which for the mathematically challenged is 490 times. Some translators insist that his response should be translated as 77 times, proving that two thousand years later we're still trying to reduce Jesus' teachings to a more manageable point.

Whatever. If you think Jesus literally meant 490 or 77, well, I guess there's nothing I can write that will prevent you from keeping score. Though I must say, I'd love to hear from you when you reach number 491 or number 78. What a book *that* would make!

See, Peter not only missed the point about forgiveness as a way of life, he also missed a basic understanding about forgiveness—as do many people who read about this encounter between Peter and Jesus. They insert words into Matthew 18:21–22 that just aren't there. Jesus says "forgive"; they read "forgive and let them back into your life and let them keep on abusing you and offending you and hurting you even if they do it 77 or 490 times." Jesus is talking about forgiveness; they're talking about reconciliation, which by now you should realize are not the same animals at all.

One of the hallmarks of Jesus' ministry was his relentless love. Biblical scholars may refute my opinion on this, but it seems to me that Jesus was making a point here about relentless love, that we have to keep on loving people by forgiving them. You can exegete any Bible verse to death, but what gives life is the spirit of the teaching and the spirit of the person

To forgive the incessant provocations of daily life—to keep on forgiving the bossy mother-in-law, the bullying husband, the nagging wife, the selfish daughter, the deceitful son—how can we do it? Only, I think, by remembering where we stand, by meaning our words when we say in our prayers each night, "Forgive us our trespasses as we forgive those who trespass against us."

—C. S. LEWIS

To realize that you are safe and happy standing at God's side, with His love encompassing you because you are forgiven; too happy to take offense any more; too much in love with life to want to be made miserable with an unforgiving heart, and knowing that now every conflict is a chance to learn more of the exceeding beauty of Love: that is worth living for, and surely worth dying to this misery-making self for.

—FLORENCE ALLSHORN

giving the teaching. Jesus was all about love, and he was all about forgiveness.

Jesus understood Peter, because he understood human nature. He understood that Peter was looking for a loophole. He wanted Jesus to give him an out. "C'mon, Jesus, get real," he seems to be saying. "You can't mean I should forgive someone, like, seven times! You've got to be kidding me!" He wants so much for Jesus to turn to him and say, "Don't be ridiculous. What ever made you think I expect you to forgive someone seven times?" The truth is, he probably didn't expect Peter to forgive anyone even once, but he knew Peter had it in him to be better than that. He was proven right, of course, though much later.

We all have it in us to be better than that. God has given us the ability to rise above the abuse, the offense, the hurt and keep on forgiving while never dismissing the impact of the pain or allowing the abuse to continue. We need to keep on forgiving, for as long as it takes.

REFLECTION

How does your ability to repeatedly forgive someone make you a better person? How does your standing with God and the forgiveness you have received in your life factor in to your ability to forgive someone else over and over again?

PRACTICE

The Qur'an has this to say about repeated forgiveness: "Forgive and overlook till God accomplish His purpose for God hath power over all things" (Qur'an II.109). That requires knowing what God's purpose is in a given situation. Is there an incident or person in your life that seems to require you to forgive over and over again? If so, ask the Spirit to show you God's purpose in that situation.

Forgive, forgive, and forgive some more. Never stop forgiving. For the temptation to project and judge will always be there as long as you are living in the body. Forgiveness is the key to peace and happiness, and gives us everything that we could possibly want.

—GERALD G. JAMPOLSKY

27 Unleashed Joy

I can't think of a single story in any religious tradition that so perfectly captures the joy of forgiveness as the story of the prodigal son does. Being a prodigal myself makes it all the more meaningful to me, but even if you can't relate to the younger son's squandering ways, you may be able to appreciate it just because it's such a good story.

The way Jesus tells it, the younger of this man's two sons was impatient to get on with his life, so he asked his father for his inheritance in advance. Soon after, he left home and blew through his money in no time. Unfortunately for him, famine struck the land where he was living, and he was forced to get a job—in a pig sty. He realized that the pigs were better off than he was, and that brought him to his senses. It also occurred to him that his father's farmhands had it pretty good. He decided to humble himself, apologize to his father, and ask him to take him on as a hired worker. Here's where the story gets really good:

When he was still a long way off, his father saw him. His heart pounding, he ran out, embraced him, and kissed him. The son started his speech: 'Father, I've sinned against God, I've sinned before you; I don't deserve to be called your son ever again.' But the father wasn't listening. He was calling to the servants.... (Luke 15:20–22, *The Message*)

Did you catch that? The father was so overjoyed at his son's return that he didn't even hear his apology. No matter. The young man was forgiven before he even asked for forgiveness. That's how quick love is to forgive.

The father then directs the servants to clean his son up, dress him in clean clothes and sandals, and place the family ring on his finger. The staff gets busy preparing a special meal in honor of his son's return. "We're going to feast! We're going to have a wonderful time!" the man said. "My son is here—given up for dead and now alive! Given up for lost and now found!" (vv. 23–24).

Can't you see the excitement? Can't you feel the joy? All is forgiven, because the son is alive! Father and son are reconciled at last, and nothing else matters!

The Bible says the angels in heaven rejoice when even one person turns to God. In the parable of the prodigal son, Jesus paints a stunning picture of what that looks like. When we're still far off—when I was still sitting in judgment of everything Christian while the biker professor droned on about forgiveness—the angels in heaven are positively jubilant, and

Joy is not gush: joy is not jolliness. Joy is simply perfect acquiescence in God's will, because the soul delights itself in God.

—AMY CARMICHAEL

A laugh, to be joyous, must flow from a joyous heart. For without kindness, there can be no true joy.

—THOMAS CARL

God is already coming to meet us more than halfway. Oh my. Oh *my*.

If God is our model for forgiveness—which God is, of course—then we should kick up our heels and sing and dance and shout for joy when a repentant friend or relative comes seeking our forgiveness. Or at least, we should feel free to do that. However we express it, we need to let joy—genuine, deep-down, regardless-of-the-circumstances joy—rock our spirit.

"The way that leads back to the Father's house after the bitter experience of sin comes through an examination of conscience, repentance and the firm intention to be converted," John Paul II said in an Ash Wednesday address in 1999, referring to this parable. "It is an interior process which changes the way one looks at reality; it makes a person realize his own frailty and it spurs the believer to throw himself into God's arms.

"This parable ... [gives] us the most concrete expression of the work of divine mercy in the human world." I couldn't have said it better.

REFLECTION

Meditate on this insight from George Seaver: "There is no situation in human life, however apparently adverse, nor any human relationship, however apparently uncongenial, that cannot be made, if God be in the heart, into a thing of perfect

Seek to cultivate a buoyant, joyous sense of the crowded kindnesses of God in your daily life.

—ALEXANDER MACLAREN

Where there is joy there is creation. Where there is no joy there is no creation: know the nature of joy.

—UPANISHADS

joy." Do you believe that? How can adverse situations be transformed into "a thing of perfect joy"?

PRACTICE

Practice being joyful. Really. You can do it. In the privacy of your own home or room, shout out a prayer of joyful praise to God. Thank God for the joy you have in your life, for everything that makes your life matter, for the people and the things you love. Remember that joy is not the same thing as happiness. Happiness is fleeting and depends on circumstances; joy is a lasting condition that no circumstances can change—at least, not for very long.

Forgiveness unleashes joy. It brings peace. It washes the slate clean. It sets all the highest values of love in motion. In a sense, forgiveness is Christianity at its highest level.

—JOHN MACARTHUR

The ineffable joy of forgiving and being forgiven forms an ecstasy that might well arouse the envy of the gods.

—ELBERT HUBBARD

28
Accepting Forgiveness

I've already told about the night I finally became reconciled to God after hearing the Bible verse about God forgiving and forgetting our sins. At the end of that meeting, I experienced a joy and freedom I had never known before. I left feeling fresh, renewed, hopeful.

And then I went home.

"Home" at the time was a room I was renting in a private house. My friends dropped me off with a cheerful "God bless you!" I hadn't been home for more than a few minutes before I started having doubts. What had just happened? Was it real? Was I crazy? Or was I really, truly forgiven? The concept boggled my mind. I got down on my knees and began praying, begging God to forgive me, over and over again. As if he hadn't.

Less than an hour later, the doorbell rang, much to the consternation of my landlady. After all, it was 1 a.m., and she wasn't accustomed to having a renter with such late visitors.

The visitors turned out to be the very friends who had taken me to the meeting earlier in the night. "We thought we'd better come back," Glenn said. "We know how it is … you get home and you start to have doubts."

For the next hour or so, Glenn and the others helped me believe that God's forgiveness was real, that I needed to accept that forgiveness and begin to live in the freedom that was now all mine. My landlady may not have been very happy that they stopped by, but I sure was. Their late-night visit made all the difference in the way I approached God from that point forward. At least for a while.

Even though I had accepted God's offer of forgiveness and reconciliation that night—oh, did I mention that the two occur simultaneously when God is the one granting forgiveness? God's got that kind of power!—in the future I would blow it time and again, with varying degrees of difficulty in accepting forgiveness afterwards. Sometimes it depended on the nature of the offense, and sometimes it just depended on my mood at the time. Still, I had to wonder: why was it so much easier to accept God's blanket forgiveness after I had been estranged from him for years than it was to accept forgiveness after we reconciled?

My guess is that I subconsciously expected to have it all together after I had made my peace with God. When it turned out that I didn't, I had a hard time accepting my failure and an even harder time believing that God wasn't totally ticked off at my evil ways. In this regard, I was no different from the early church; the reality that a person could still commit a sin after

> Genuine forgiveness is participation, reunion overcoming the powers of estrangement.... We cannot love unless we have accepted forgiveness, and the deeper our experience of forgiveness is, the greater is our love.
>
> —PAUL TILLICH

baptism was utterly astonishing to the early believers, and they had to figure out what that meant in terms of God's forgiveness and reconciling with the rest of the church community.

I've derived a great deal of comfort from something the evangelist Luis Palau once said: "God isn't disillusioned with us. He never had any illusions to begin with."[12] Isn't that a wonderful thought? Of course God never expected me to be perfect! That's why he set up a procedure for seeking and attaining forgiveness in the first place.

In the last chapter we looked at the parable of the prodigal son. Remember how the sight of his son affected the father? And the kid hadn't even apologized yet! But the father was so overjoyed at his son's return that he didn't need an explanation; his son had returned! Imagine how much joy it brings to God when we return *and* repent. Would God withhold forgiveness? I think not. I think that what we have here, in situations where we find it difficult to accept God's forgiveness, is in reality a failure to forgive ourselves.

Forgiveness is a gift from God. By not accepting it—by believing that there are strings attached and that God is going to yank the gift right out of our hands—we're losing out on the freedom that comes with forgiveness and the restored relationship we can have with God. We don't need to do anything other than accept the gift. There's nothing more we *can* do; it's all been done for us.

When it comes right down to it, accepting God's forgiveness is an act of faith. If we continue to doubt whether we're forgiven, we need to ask for the faith to believe that we are.

> Without being forgiven, released from the consequences of what we have done, our capacity to act would, as it were, be confined to a single deed from which we could never recover; we would remain the victims of its consequences forever, not unlike the sorcerer's apprentice, who lacked the magic formula to break the spell.
>
> —HANNAH ARENDT

REFLECTION

Reflect on whether you believe God has forgiven you. How do you perceive God's gift of forgiveness? Are there strings attached? If so, what do those strings represent? Ask God to give you an accurate picture of what the gift of forgiveness looks like.

PRACTICE

Write out a prayer to God in which you express your gratitude for his offer of forgiveness. Clearly state that you are accepting the offer and that you understand there are no conditions attached. Even so, out of gratitude indicate your resolve to turn away from the sin that once separated you from God. End by thanking God for your restored relationship.

Most people feel unworthy of forgiveness.

—LUIS PALAU

Now when sins have been forgiven, there is no need to offer any more sacrifices.

—HEBREWS 10:18
(NLT)

29

Sharing the Blame

Author Cathy Lechner tells of an amusing incident that happened following a luncheon she attended with a group of women. Crowded in the back seat of a car on the way back to the hotel where the women were staying, Cathy began to detect the unmistakable odor of garlic. Looking around at the other women in the car, she realized that whoever the culprit was, she was oblivious to the offensive smell in the back seat.

Cathy tried everything she could to avoid the odor, which seemed to be getting stronger with each passing mile. She rolled down the window. She twisted her head this way and that, all to no avail. And then, something caught her attention. There it was, the obvious source of the garlic smell—a piece of Caesar dressing-soaked lettuce lodged firmly in her own cleavage. She was the one who was stinking up the car.

Sometimes, we have to admit that we're the one stinking up a situation. We're so quick to point the finger at the other guy and so slow to acknowledge our own blame. But in many cases where someone has done us wrong, we've contributed to the offensive situation in some way and to some degree. We'd like to believe that the share of the blame is generally split 90 percent to 10 percent, in our favor, of course. But the truth is, sometimes we contribute a whole lot more than 10 percent.

We need to come clean about what is our fault, for a number of reasons. First, we're not fooling God about our supposed innocence, and second, we have to stop trying to fool ourselves. A clean conscience before God and within ourselves is invaluable in achieving the peace we say we want. Third, the person who offended us is most likely well aware of our contribution to the rift between us; we need to be prepared to own up to our guilt in the event that our offender tries to make a federal case out of it while we're trying to make peace with him.

Remember Janet, whose husband died and left her with a truckload of grief and guilt? One of the realities Janet had to face was that during those last five years of their marriage, the years when Bill basically dropped the ball, she was a royal pain to live with. The family's myriad problems were largely her fault, and while Bill could have been more supportive and helpful, she had to admit that she had rebuffed his support and help for so long that it was no wonder he stopped offering both. We'll call that one 75 percent to 25 percent in Janet's favor, mainly because she's my friend.

And then there's the philandering Mark and the longsuffering Cathy, the couple who divorced and remarried four years later. Cathy realized that she had contributed to their marital problems by not confronting Mark early on about his late nights

We admit, O God, how bad we've lived, and our ancestors, how bad they were. We've sinned, they've sinned, we've all sinned against you!

—JEREMIAH 14:20
(THE MESSAGE)

133

and by focusing her attention on her children as a way of avoiding the many signs of trouble all around her. This one? Roughly 99 percent Mark, 1 percent Cathy. I'm feeling generous.

Graduates of twelve-step programs—at least, those who actually *do* the program—understand the concept of admitting faults better than most of us do. Overcoming an addiction is an exceedingly difficult thing to do, and those who are determined to do it don't let themselves off the hook all that lightly. Among the twelve steps are taking a moral inventory of our lives, admitting our faults to God and others, making amends wherever possible, and allowing God to make the necessary changes in our lives. To a recovering addict, it makes no difference whether she is 60 percent to blame or just 10 percent. Her contribution to the problem needs to be confessed and corrected, regardless of who was most at fault.

It's not easy for some of us to admit we're wrong, especially when someone else is a whole lot more wrong. Still, we have to look closely at ourselves and recognize that sometimes, we're the ones stinking up the back seat of the car. It's the only way we can clean up our lives and get rid of the stench.

> But if we confess our sins to him, he is faithful and just to forgive us and to cleanse us from every wrong.
>
> **—1 John 1:9 (NLT)**

REFLECTION

Are you defensive? Many people are without realizing the extent to which they fail to assume responsibility for their own behavior. If your offender were to turn the tables on you and draw attention to your share of the blame, would you be prepared to come clean with him, admitting your fault while gently shifting the focus back to the matter at hand—your forgiveness or attempt at reconciliation?

PRACTICE

So maybe you're not an addict. It's unfortunate that people resist a really good idea or practice just because it's associated with something they perceive to be unpleasant or shameful. The Twelve Steps of Alcoholics Anonymous are a powerful tool for anyone to use. Here they are; I've bracketed wording that you may want to customize for your own situation:

1. We admitted we were powerless [over alcohol]—that our lives had become unmanageable.

2. Came to believe that a Power greater than ourselves could restore us to sanity.

3. Made a decision to turn our will and our lives over to the care of God as we understood Him.

4. Made a searching and fearless moral inventory of ourselves.

5. Admitted to God, to ourselves and to another human being the exact nature of our wrongs.

6. Were entirely ready to have God remove all these defects of character.

Contrition is most difficult when it requires admitting we were wrong—which is seldom fun to do, and never as enjoyable as reveling in being right. Sometimes, facing up to our own fault is excruciating.

—M. BLAINE SMITH

7. Humbly asked Him to remove our shortcomings.

8. Made a list of all persons we had harmed, and became willing to make amends to them all.

9. Made direct amends to such people wherever possible, except when to do so would injure them or others.

10. Continued to take personal inventory and when we were wrong promptly admitted it.

11. Sought through prayer and meditation to improve our conscious contact with God, as we understood Him, praying only for knowledge of His will for us and the power to carry that out.

12. Having had a spiritual awakening as the result of these steps, we tried to carry this message to [alcoholics], and to practice these principles in all our affairs.

Give them grace, when they hurt each other, to recognize and acknowledge their fault, and to seek each other's forgiveness and yours. Amen.

—FROM THE MARRIAGE LITURGY OF *THE BOOK OF COMMON PRAYER*

Can We Forgive God?

When I first started working on this project, one of the proposed subtitles for the book was *Forgiving Others, Ourselves and God.* My knee-jerk reaction was this: we can't forgive God. So I nixed that wording, convinced that the very idea of forgiving God bordered on blasphemy.

I've since come to understand what people actually mean when they say they've forgiven God—or when I hear irreverent pop singer Morrissey singing "I Have Forgiven Jesus" for the umpteenth time. I realized that the problem was one of multiple definitions of a single term. I heard one thing in the words "forgiving God"; other people heard, and meant, something entirely different. In this case, I have to admit I was pretty dense, which is something I don't readily admit.

My thinking had been faulty from the get-go. I envisioned "forgiving God" as absolving him of sin, the way he forgives us by absolving us of sin. Well, now, really—it's no wonder I was so averse to the idea. If I had that kind of power, I'd have been ruling the world a long time ago.

What other people meant by forgiving God was far more sane and reasonable. In situations where no human being can be held responsible for a tragedy, victims need a place to direct their anger. God becomes a convenient and logical target—especially when an "act of God" takes a loved one's life. Who else is there to blame for an avalanche, an earthquake, a tsunami?

Sometimes the line between God and a person's loss is even more direct. A young boy falls from a tree and snaps his neck. A toddler manages to crawl through a fence and drowns in the pool on the other side. A young pastor and fellow author is electrocuted when he unthinkingly reaches for a microphone as he's performing a baptism. Couldn't God have prevented Kyle Lake from grabbing an electrical cord while standing in shoulder-high water? How could God allow him to suffer electrocution in front of eight hundred people, including his wife and the brand-new believer he was about to baptize?

How can we possibly make sense out of tragedies like that? We can't. All we can do, if we're somewhat distanced from the situation, is acknowledge that there are some things that we'll never understand.

But for the survivors—that's another story entirely. I don't know if Kyle's wife ever had a moment when she genuinely "blamed" God, but I'm guessing that more than once Jen questioned why God allowed such a horrible thing to happen. The survivors of tragic accidents like Kyle's have no human being to blame, no one they can vent their anger on. They run the very

> Should we forgive God? Perhaps. Must we forgive God? No. But if it helps reconcile you to God and gives you peace, then feel free to do so.
>
> —DAVID SIELAFF

real risk of sinking into clinical depression, one of the results of bottling up all that anger. I have a feeling God would rather be blamed than see that happen.

One thing I know for sure—God is big enough to take your blame, your rage, your outrage. I've duked it out with him so many times that it's a wonder we're on speaking terms these days. It has never occurred to me to forgive God, though; I seem to always end up asking God to forgive me for blaming him for all my troubles, most of which are of my own making.

But blaming God poses another problem—estrangement. As long as you are blaming God, the two of you can't very well have a healthy relationship. Only through forgiveness can you be reconciled to God again, so there you go. We've come right back to forgiveness once again.

Once you've enjoyed a healthy, loving relationship with God, alienation from him is never fun. It's much better to vent your anger over a horrible loss than to live with the frustration and misery of trying to go it alone. Forgive God and get over it. Living apart from the Spirit is just not worth it.

REFLECTION

How do you make sense of the senseless tragedies you either have experienced or have heard about? Do you believe that God is really in control? Do you tend to blame God when bad things happen and there's no one else to blame? How has that affected your relationship with God?

> Frustrated by our inability to pin down a reason for our pain, which we are quick to see as unjustified and undeserved, we rebel against it and accuse God…. Still, it is fruitless to stay angry at God. We can hold him responsible for hurting us, but he cannot very well apologize.
>
> —JOHANN CHRISTOPH ARNOLD

> "My thoughts are completely different from yours," says the Lord. "And my ways are far beyond anything you could imagine. For just as the heavens are higher than the earth, so are my ways higher than your ways and my thoughts higher than your thoughts."
> **—ISAIAH 55:8–9 (NLT)**

PRACTICE

Maybe you're like me—the thought of "forgiving God" just doesn't sit well with you. Still, you have unresolved issues with God that you'd like to get cleared up. Do what I do—let him have it. Vent your anger to God. Be specific—very specific. Make this one an encounter with God of epic proportions. Hold nothing back. Just be prepared to be humbled. Ask God's forgiveness for yelling so loud, trust that you will eventually get the answers you feel you deserve, and get on with your life and your relationship with the Spirit.

31
Tell Your Story

In the spring of 1995, a Nigerian man named Raymond embarked on something of a sacred journey that would take him to a half-dozen nations across the African continent. His mission: to say goodbye to those friends and family members who had meant the most to him throughout his life. At the age of forty-two, Raymond was dying—dying of despair. He had seen too much hatred and strife, too much bloodshed and violence, too much oppression and warfare. It was time to die, and by his own hand.

Among the last faces he wanted to see on earth was that of his brother in Kenya, and so he chose Nairobi as the final stop on his pilgrimage. He arrived late at night and decided to wait until morning to tell his brother why he had come and what he intended to do when he left. Though he was at peace with his decision to commit suicide, he found himself restless and sleepless, so he absentmindedly picked up a magazine from the bedside table and began leafing through it.

Whatever it was that happened over the next hour or so can only be described as miraculous. Though I never learned the exact details of Raymond's reading session, I do know this: Raymond did not commit suicide the next day or any other day, because in the pages of that magazine he discovered a story of forgiveness and reconciliation so powerful that it infused his spirit with *hope*—something he had lost decades earlier.

The magazine was the January 1995 of *Charisma,* where I worked as news editor at the time. Every year, the staff compiled a special edition dubbed "Holy Spirit Around the World," highlighting evidence of God's activity in the global hot spots of the previous year. In this case, the year was 1994, and one of the articles featured the aftermath of the horrendous civil strife in Rwanda in which the warring Hutus and Tutsis brutally slaughtered each other, the bodies of nearly a million men, women, and children piled into mass graves that littered the countryside. Millions more Rwandans flooded into neighboring countries seeking refuge. No group of people was spared; among the dead were nearly five hundred Catholic priests and religious and an undetermined number of Protestant clergy, many killed in their churches.

Months after the massacre ended, church services slowly began to be held again. Numb with grief and shock, worshippers at one such service listened as a guest preacher began to speak. Their own pastor was still living in a refugee camp in Zaire. The visiting preacher's sermon topic was forgiveness.

Forgiveness? *Forgiveness?* These people had witnessed unimaginable cruelty. One tribe had routinely hacked off the

Never does the human soul appear so strong and noble as when it forgoes revenge and dares to forgive an injury.

—EDWIN HUBBELL CHAPIN

legs of their enemies to literally cut them down to size before murdering them. Children as young as eight were forced at gunpoint to kill their neighbors. How could this man—this *guest preacher*—dare to speak to them about forgiveness?

Not easily, I'm sure. But also not without significant grounds, because the speaker had suffered tremendous loss as well. Among the victims of the war were nearly seventy members of his extended family. And he had forgiven every one of their murderers, though he didn't know their names—or their fate.

That and other stories of forgiveness in the face of inconceivable carnage provided Raymond with undeniable evidence of the power of God's grace. Equally compelling were the accounts of reconciliation between individual Hutu and Tutsi survivors—and the ongoing effort toward national reconciliation and the rebuilding of a shattered country.

If members of two groups who detested each other so much could even talk about reconciliation, much less accomplish it, there was indeed cause for Raymond to believe in hope again. And if love could defeat such overwhelming hatred, there was cause for Raymond to believe in love again. Right there in his brother's guest room, Raymond was himself overcome by love—the love of God. He forgave those who had robbed him of the joy of life and decided that life was in fact worth living.

How do I know so much about a man I've never met, a man who lives on a continent I've never visited? Raymond told his story in a letter he sent to me in the summer of 1995, eight months after relief worker Reg Reimer and I had collaborated on the story about Rwanda. Raymond wanted to thank us for

> The practice of forgiveness is our most important contribution to the healing of the world.
>
> —MARIANNE WILLIAMSON

143

telling the world about the power of forgiveness and reconciliation and for saving his life in the process.

Well! There I was, sitting in a cubicle in the editorial department of a magazine with maybe two hundred thousand subscribers—interviewing, editing, writing, weekday after long weekday—most days wondering if anybody ever really read anything I wrote. And then Raymond's letter arrived.

Do we need to tell our stories of forgiveness and reconciliation? You bet we do. Follow the trail of just these few stories and the impact they had: Survivors of the civil war in Rwanda told Reg how they were able to forgive their enemies and be reconciled to them; Reg and I repeated those stories in print for the readers of *Charisma*; Raymond told us how those stories saved his life; and—hallelujah!—Raymond's story helped validate the worthiness of my life's work.

Our stories help us heal. Our stories help others heal. Our stories, taken together, help the world heal—little by little, to be sure. But I'd rather contribute a little healing than none at all.

REFLECTION

Your life is probably blessedly free of genuine enemies—the kind of murderous adversaries that the Rwandans faced in 1994 and that many people throughout the world continue to face today. Consider what it would be like to live in such an environment and to make a conscious decision to forgive your enemies in advance, before you even knew the kind of brutal-

Do not say, "I'll do to him as he has done to me; I'll pay that man back for what he did."

—PROVERBS 24:29
(NIV)

ity they would inflict on you. How do you think that would affect the way you lived your life, especially with regard to the level of fear you would experience?

PRACTICE

Tell your story of forgiveness and reconciliation—any story. It could be one that involved you personally or one you witnessed that had a significant impact on your life. Write it down in as much detail as you can recall. Then share that story with someone else. Depending on the circumstances and the nature of the story, you may want to rework it as a reflection for a congregational newsletter or even submit it for publication to an appropriate magazine. And please send a copy to me at misfit@marciaford.com.

We have been sent to speak for Christ. It is as if God is calling to you through us. We speak for Christ when we beg you to be at peace with God.

—2 CORINTHIANS 5:20 (NLT)

Afterword

Among the Athabaskan people of Alaska's Yukon Territory there's a centuries-old legend about two elderly women who were abandoned and left to fend for themselves during a time of famine. Over many generations tales had been told of similar situations. Forced to seek out a new hunting ground, a tribe would abandon its weakest members, leaving them to face a certain and terrifying death by starvation—or worse. But such a radical action had not been seen for some time. And so, when the tribal chief announced his decision to leave Sa' and Ch'idzigyaak behind, the two old women were stunned.

Determined not to show their feelings, Sa' and Ch'idzigyaak stared straight ahead as the tribe prepared to leave. Ch'idzigyaak felt all the more betrayed; among those walking away from her were her own daughter and grandson. The boy she could forgive; her daughter, she could not. Ch'idzigyaak had taught her to be strong and courageous, to fight injustice and defend the helpless. Ozhii had not learned her lessons well.

Few people can even imagine the hardships the two women faced as they struggled to survive the frigid Arctic winter. But the skills they had learned in their earlier years—long before they came to depend on a younger generation to care for them in their old age—returned to them. Recalling a favorable campsite near a creek, they set out to find the nearly forgotten setting. Along the way, they trapped, they skinned, they fished, though the pain in their fragile joints and atrophied muscles often begged them to give up, to lie down and die.

But they did not lie down and die. By spring, they found the old campsite, along with enough fish, game, and berries to set aside a significant store for the brutal winter to come. They built a warm and snug tent from deer hides and gathered more than enough wood to keep their fires glowing during the long Alaskan winter. They were confident they would survive the subzero weather in relative comfort.

Still, the sting of their betrayal continued to cause them pain. And so, when late one night they heard a voice in the distance calling their names, Sa' and Ch'idzigyaak at first did not respond. Only when they determined that their discovery was inevitable did they call in return. An elderly scout from their tribe, skilled not only in tracking but also in trusting his intuition, had been searching for them for days after deciding that they would have been smart and resilient enough to seek out the old campsite.

The tribe at first kept its distance from the two old women, respecting their wish to be left alone. The women no longer trusted the tribe, and it would take time for their wounds to heal. After a while, Sa' and Ch'idzigyaak sent food from their stores to the tribe, whose numbers had dwindled due to the famine that plagued the land they hunted. Their own hardship had softened their hearts toward those who had blindly followed the tribal chief's decision to abandon them a year earlier.

Weeks passed. One day, Ch'idzigyaak's grandson appeared at her campsite. There was never any question that she had freely and completely forgiven him long before. Their joyous reunion, however, was tainted by an unasked question that hung in the air between them. What about Ozhii? Why had she left Ch'idzigyaak behind? And why had she not come to visit her mother in the weeks since the scout had discovered her?

Ch'idzigyaak eventually summoned the courage to ask about Ozhii. Was her daughter so callous that she had no concern for her mother? Was she too proud to even ask about her? *Never!* her grandson Shruh insisted. She was ashamed that she had allowed hunger to rob her of the strength to fight for her mother the previous year. She had no right to expect her mother's forgiveness. She had no reason to hope that they would ever be reconciled.

Upon returning to camp, Shruh assured Ozhii that her mother had indeed forgiven her. Time had given Ch'idzigyaak a deeper insight into the predicament her daughter had faced. To rebel against the chief by defending her mother was to risk not only her own death but that of her mother and her son as well. Encouraged by Shruh's report, Ozhii set out for Ch'idzigyaak's campsite—but with a fair amount of trepidation. What if he was wrong?

Ozhii need not have worried. At the sight of her daughter, Ch'idzigyaak held out her arms to embrace her, tears streaming down her weather-lined cheeks. Yes, Ch'idzigyaak had forgiven Ozhii, freely and completely. From that time forward, the Athabaskan people never again abandoned one of their own. The memory of the wrong they had done to Sa' and Ch'idzigyaak would not permit them to.

Why did I choose this ancient legend to end our discussion of forgiveness and reconciliation? Surely a more contemporary example would have sufficed. Well, that's true, but then I wouldn't have been able to indulge my passion for all things Alaskan. But mainly, I chose to use this story, which I adapted from Velma Wallis's *Two Old Women*, because it contains not only a number of concepts we've already explored but also one unexplored possibility that offers hope that a greater good really can result from injustice.

But first, the familiar concepts. For one, the offense needs to be a clear-cut, personal wrong. Your neighbor Jason can get on your nerves and generally drive you nuts, but that's not a clear-cut wrong. In the Alaska story, the tribal chief committed a clear-cut, personal wrong against Sa' and Ch'idzigyaak. In Ch'idzigyaak's mind, so did her daughter. To both Sa' and Ch'idzigyaak, the entire tribe had wronged them.

A second concept is that the wrong that was committed must result in some measure of estrangement, whether physical or emotional. If someone has supposedly wronged you but the offense barely made a blip on your relational radar screen, then either the offense wasn't all that offensive or you've already—perhaps unknowingly—forgiven the offender. The estrangement of Sa' and Ch'idzigyaak from the tribe, and from Ch'idzigyaak's family, was both physical and emotional. And for a year, it also appeared to be final. The two women had no reason to believe they would see their tribe again. The tribe had no reason to believe that the two frail, elderly women were still alive.

A third indication of the potential for forgiveness is that the offended person's heart begins to soften—even if only slightly—toward the offender. This, as we've seen, is the point at which many people get stuck. When we've been wronged, it's hard to accept it when we feel the first inklings of compassion for our offender. Sa' and Ch'idzigyaak experienced those first inklings when they began to identify with the plight of their people. The two women could easily have died of starvation; they knew firsthand how extreme hunger and deprivation felt. When they discovered that innocent children had been among those who had died during the famine, they shared their food with the tribe.

Then there's the possibility of reconciliation, which needs to be considered carefully and judiciously. The women handled the prospect of reconciliation with wisdom. The trust they once had in the tribe was shattered the day their people left them behind. The women took slow and careful steps toward a reconciliation that no one was certain would take place until it actually occurred. They laid down the ground rules, requiring the tribe to keep their distance and have only limited contact with them at first. The offenders showed their willingness to be reconciled by agreeing to the women's terms. They simply could have overpowered the women and made off with all their food. Instead, they chose to prove their trustworthiness by showing the respect they had failed to show a year earlier.

And now we come to that unexplored final element, one that offers hope for humanity in the midst of injustice. Remember the myth of "forgive and forget"? As the forgiver, you "forget" not by erasing your memory but by choosing not to dwell on the offense. But look at the twist in this story: It's a tale of "be forgiven and never forget." The clan intentionally *remembered* the injustice they had perpetrated, as a way of insuring that such an offense would never be committed again.

Imagine what would happen if everyone you have forgiven chose to intentionally remember their acts of injustice or betrayal or downright meanness, as a way of insuring that they never behave that way again. What if—what if the offender proves to be a better person, all because of the forgiveness you extended?

One can only hope.

Acknowledgments

My thanks go to:

- Maura Shaw, my editor at SkyLight Paths, who suggested this project to me and encouraged me along the way.

- Palmer Jones, my editor at Explorefaith.org, who invited to me to write about forgiveness for the website; that article caught Maura's attention and resulted in this book.

- The many people in my life who have taught me priceless lessons on forgiveness. Some are named; some of the unnamed are better left that way, since they taught me, by their negative example, what *not* to do. Most of the unnamed, however, are anonymous people who demonstrated forgiveness and reconciliation in their everyday lives in ways that were memorable, even if their names were not.

- The entire team at SkyLight Paths. What a delightful experience this has been!

Credits

Chapter 5 is adapted from a column that first appeared on the website www.explorefaith.org.

Scripture marked NAS is taken from the New American Standard Bible, copyright 1960, 1962, 1963, 1968, 1971, 1972, 1973, 1975, 1977, 1995 by The Lockman Foundation. Used by permission.

Scripture marked NCV is taken from the New Century Version, copyright 1987, 1988, 1991 by Word Publishing, a division of Thomas Nelson, Inc. All rights reserved. Used by permission.

Scripture marked NKJV is taken from the New King James Version, copyright 1982 by Thomas Nelson Inc. Used by permission. All rights reserved.

Scripture marked NLT is taken from the Holy Bible, New Living Translation, copyright 1996. Used by permission of Tyndale House Publishers. All rights reserved.

Scripture marked NRSV is taken from the New Revised Standard Version, copyright 1989, Division of Christian Education of the National Council of the Churches of Christ in the United States of America. All rights reserved. Used with permission.

Scripture marked *The Message* is from *The Message: The Bible in Contemporary Language,* copyright 2002 by Eugene Peterson. Used with permission of NavPress Publishing Group. All rights reserved.

The Twelve Steps are reprinted with permission of Alcoholics Anonymous World Services, Inc. (A.A.W.S.). Permission to reprint the Twelve Steps does not mean that A.A.W.S. has reviewed or approved the contents of this publication, or that A.A.W.S. necessarily agrees with the views expressed herein. A.A. is a program of recovery from alcoholism *only*—use of the Twelve Steps in connection with programs and activities which are patterned after A.A., but which address other problems, or in any other non-A.A. context, does not imply otherwise. Additionally, while A.A. is a spiritual program, A.A. is not a religious program. Thus, A.A. is not affiliated or allied with any sect, denomination, or specific religious belief.

Notes

1. Martin Luther King Jr., *Strength to Love* (New York: Harper & Row, 1963), 40.

2. Marian Anderson, *My Lord, What a Morning: An Autobiography* (New York: Viking Press, 1956), ch. 28. Quoted on www.bartleby.com, citing Andrews, Robert, Mary Biggs and Michael Seidel, et al. *The Columbia World of Quotations* (New York: Columbia University Press, 1996), Quote 3500.

3. Christopher Titmuss, *Light on Enlightenment: Revolutionary Teachings on the Inner Life* (Boston: Shambhala, 1999), 180.

4. Diane K. Obson, ed., *A Joseph Campbell Companion: Reflections on the Art of Living* (New York: HarperCollins, 1991), 53.

5. Lewis B. Smedes, *The Art of Forgiving: When You Need to Forgive and Don't Know How* (Nashville: Moorings, 1996).

6. Smedes, *The Art of Forgiving*.

7. Charles Fillmore, quoted on www.quotelady.com/subjects/ forgiveness.html.

8. Personal notes taken at a talk given by George Barna at the International Christian Retail Show, Denver, Colorado, July, 2005.

9. Henry Wadsworth Longfellow, quoted on www.quotedb.com/ quotes/1825.

10. Charles Stanley, *The Gift of Forgiveness*.

11. Personal notes taken during Bill Gothard's "Institute in Basic Youth Conflicts" seminars, which were held annually in churches and other venues throughout the country in the 1970s.

12. Luis Palau, "Does God Make a Difference?" (sermon, available on www.csec.org).

Suggestions for Further Reading

Campbell, Joseph. *The Hero with a Thousand Faces.* 2nd ed. Princeton, NJ: Princeton University Press, 1968.

Dyja, Thomas. *Life-Changing Stories of Forgiving and Being Forgiven.* New York: Marlowe, 2001.

Elkins, Dov Peretz. *Rosh Hashanah Readings: Inspiration, Information and Contemplation.* Woodstock, VT: Jewish Lights, 2010.

———. *Yom Kippur Readings: Inspiration, Information and Contemplation.* Woodstock, VT: Jewish Lights, 2010.

Flanigan, Beverly. *Forgiving Yourself: A Step-by-Step Guide to Finding Peace with Your Mistakes and Getting On with Your Life.* New York: Macmillan, 1996.

Ford, Marcia. *Finding Hope: Cultivating God's Gift of a Hopeful Spirit.* Woodstock, VT: SkyLight Paths, 2007.

Ketterman, Grace H., and David Hazard. *When You Can't Say "I Forgive You": Breaking the Bonds of Anger and Hurt.* Colorado Springs: NavPress, 2000.

Lindahl, Kay. *The Sacred Art of Listening: Forty Reflections for Cultivating a Spiritual Practice.* Woodstock, VT: SkyLight Paths, 2002.

Meyer, Joyce. *The Power of Forgiveness: Keep Your Heart Free.* New York: Warner Books, 2003.

Rutledge, Thom. *The Self-Forgiveness Handbook: A Practical and Empowering Guide.* Oakland, CA: New Harbinger, 1997.

Schmidt, Doug. *The Prayer of Revenge: Forgiveness in the Face of Injustice.* Colorado Springs: Cook Communications, 2003.

Shults, F. LeRon, and Steven J. Sandage. *The Faces of Forgiveness: Searching for Wholeness and Salvation.* Grand Rapids, MI: Baker Book House, 2003.

Simon, Sidney B., and Suzanne Simon. *Forgiveness: How to Make Peace with Your Past and Get On with Your Life.* New York: Warner Books, 1990.

Smedes, Lewis B. *Forgive and Forget: Healing the Hurts We Don't Deserve.* San Francisco: HarperSanFrancisco, 1984.

———. *The Art of Forgiving: When You Need to Forgive and Don't Know How.* Nashville: Moorings, 1996.

Spring, Janis Abrahms, with Michael Spring. *How Can I Forgive You? The Courage to Forgive, the Freedom Not To.* New York: HarperCollins, 2004.

Stanley, Charles F. *The Gift of Forgiveness.* Nashville: Thomas Nelson, 1991.

ten Boom, Corrie, with John and Elizabeth Sherrill. *The Hiding Place.* Boston: G. K. Hall, 1973.

Tobin, Eamon. *How to Forgive Yourself and Others: Steps to Reconciliation.* Rev. ed. Liguori, MO: Liguori Publications, 1993.

Wallis, Velma. *Two Old Women: An Alaska Legend of Betrayal, Courage, and Survival.* New York: HarperPerennial, 1993.

Williamson, Marianne. *Illuminata: A Return to Prayer.* New York: Riverhead Books, 1995.

Worthington, Everett L., Jr. *Forgiving and Reconciling: Bridges to Wholeness and Hope.* Downers Grove, IL: InterVarsity Press, 2003.

Adam & Eve's New Day

by Sandy Eisenberg Sasso; Full-color illus. by Joani Keller Rothenberg

A lesson in hope for every child who has worried about what comes next. Abridged from *Adam & Eve's First Sunset*.

5 x 5, 24 pp, Full-color illus., Board Book, 978-1-59473-205-8 **$7.99** *For ages 0–4*

How Did the Animals Help God?

by Nancy Sohn Swartz; Full-color illus. by Melanie Hall

God asks all of nature to offer gifts to humankind—with a promise that they will care for creation in return. Abridged from *In Our Image*.

5 x 5, 24 pp, Full-color illus., Board Book, 978-1-59473-044-3 **$7.99** *For ages 0–4*

How Does God Make Things Happen?

by Lawrence and Karen Kushner; Full-color illus. by Dawn W. Majewski

A charming invitation for young children to explore how God makes things happen in our world. Abridged from *Because Nothing Looks Like God*.

5 x 5, 24 pp, Full-color illus., Board Book, 978-1-893361-24-9 **$7.95** *For ages 0–4*

What Does God Look Like?

by Lawrence and Karen Kushner; Full-color illus. by Dawn W. Majewski

A simple way for young children to explore the ways that we "see" God. Abridged from *Because Nothing Looks Like God*.

5 x 5, 24 pp, Full-color illus., Board Book, 978-1-893361-23-2 **$7.99** *For ages 0–4*

What Is God's Name?

by Sandy Eisenberg Sasso; Full-color illus. by Phoebe Stone

Everyone and everything in the world has a name. What is God's name? Abridged from the award-winning *In God's Name*.

5 x 5, 24 pp, Full-color illus., Board Book, 978-1-893361-10-2 **$7.99** *For ages 0–4*

Where Is God?

by Lawrence and Karen Kushner; Full-color illus. by Dawn W. Majewski

A gentle way for young children to explore how God is with us every day, in every way. Abridged from *Because Nothing Looks Like God*.

5 x 5, 24 pp, Full-color illus., Board Book, 978-1-893361-17-1 **$7.99** *For ages 0–4*

Or phone, fax, mail or e-mail to: SKYLIGHT PATHS Publishing
Sunset Farm Offices, Route 4 • P.O. Box 237 • Woodstock, Vermont 05091
Tel: (802) 457-4000 • Fax: (802) 457-4004 • www.skylightpaths.com
Credit card orders: **(800) 962-4544** (8:30AM–5:30PM ET Monday–Friday)

Generous discounts on quantity orders. SATISFACTION GUARANTEED. Prices subject to change.

Children's Spirituality

Remembering My Grandparent: A Kid's Own Grief Workbook in the Christian Tradition
by Nechama Liss-Levinson, PhD, and Rev. Molly Phinney Baskette, MDiv
8 x 10, 48 pp, 2-color text, HC, 978-1-59473-212-6 $16.99 For ages 7 & up

Does God Ever Sleep? *by Joan Sauro, CSJ*
A charming nighttime reminder that God is always present in our lives.
10 x 8½, 32 pp, Full-color photos, Quality PB, 978-1-59473-110-5 **$8.99** *For ages 3–6*

Does God Forgive Me? *by August Gold; Full-color photos by Diane Hardy Waller*
Gently shows how God forgives all that we do if we are truly sorry.
10 x 8½, 32 pp, Full-color photos, Quality PB, 978-1-59473-142-6 **$8.99** *For ages 3–6*

God Said Amen *by Sandy Eisenberg Sasso; Full-color illus. by Avi Katz*
A warm and inspiring tale that shows us that we need only reach out to each other to find the answers to our prayers.
9 x 12, 32 pp, Full-color illus., HC, 978-1-58023-080-3 **$16.95*** *For ages 4 & up*

How Does God Listen? *by Kay Lindahl; Full-color photos by Cynthia Maloney*
How do we know when God is listening to us? Children will find the answers to these questions as they engage their senses while the story unfolds, learning how God listens in the wind, waves, clouds, hot chocolate, perfume, our tears and our laughter.
10 x 8½, 32 pp, Full-color photos, Quality PB, 978-1-59473-084-9 **$8.99** *For ages 3–6*

In God's Hands *by Lawrence Kushner and Gary Schmidt; Full-color illus. by Matthew J. Baek*
9 x 12, 32 pp, Full-color illus., HC, 978-1-58023-224-1 **$16.99*** *For ages 5 & up*

In God's Name *by Sandy Eisenberg Sasso; Full-color illus. by Phoebe Stone*
Like an ancient myth in its poetic text and vibrant illustrations, this award-winning modern fable about the search for God's name celebrates the diversity and, at the same time, the unity of all the people of the world.
9 x 12, 32 pp, Full-color illus., HC, 978-1-879045-26-2 **$16.99*** *For ages 4 & up*

Also available in Spanish: **El nombre de Dios**
9 x 12, 32 pp, Full-color illus., HC, 978-1-893361-63-8 **$16.95**

In Our Image: God's First Creatures
by Nancy Sohn Swartz; Full-color illus. by Melanie Hall
A playful new twist on the Genesis story—from the perspective of the animals. Celebrates the interconnectedness of nature and the harmony of all living things.
9 x 12, 32 pp, Full-color illus., HC, 978-1-879045-99-6 **$16.95*** *For ages 4 & up*

Noah's Wife: The Story of Naamah
by Sandy Eisenberg Sasso; Full-color illus. by Bethanne Andersen
Opens young readers' religious imaginations to new ideas about the well-known story of the Flood. When God tells Noah to bring the animals of the world onto the ark, God also calls on Naamah, Noah's wife, to save each plant on Earth.
9 x 12, 32 pp, Full-color illus., HC, 978-1-58023-134-3 **$16.95*** *For ages 4 & up*

Also available: **Naamah:** Noah's Wife (A Board Book)
by Sandy Eisenberg Sasso; Full-color illus. by Bethanne Andersen
5 x 5, 24 pp, Full-color illus., Board Book, 978-1-893361-56-0 **$7.95** *For ages 0–4*

Where Does God Live? *by August Gold and Matthew J. Perlman*
Helps children and their parents find God in the world around us with simple, practical examples children can relate to. 10 x 8½, 32 pp, Full-color photos, Quality PB, 978-1-893361-39-3 **$8.99** *For ages 3–6*

* A book from Jewish Lights, SkyLight Paths' sister imprint

Bible Stories / Folktales

Abraham's Bind & Other Bible Tales of Trickery, Folly, Mercy and Love *by Michael J. Caduto*
New retellings of episodes in the lives of familiar biblical characters explore relevant life lessons.
6 x 9, 224 pp, HC, 978-1-59473-186-0 **$19.99**

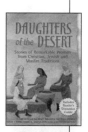

Daughters of the Desert: Stories of Remarkable Women from Christian, Jewish and Muslim Traditions
by Claire Rudolf Murphy, Meghan Nuttall Sayres, Mary Cronk Farrell, Sarah Conover and Betsy Wharton
Breathes new life into the old tales of our female ancestors in faith. Uses traditional scriptural passages as starting points, then with vivid detail fills in historical context and place. Chapters reveal the voices of Sarah, Hagar, Huldah, Esther, Salome, Mary Magdalene, Lydia, Khadija, Fatima and many more. Historical fiction ideal for readers of all ages.
5½ x 8½, 192 pp, Quality PB, 978-1-59473-106-8 **$14.99** Inc. reader's discussion guide, HC, 978-1-893361-72-0 **$19.95**

The Triumph of Eve & Other Subversive Bible Tales
by Matt Biers-Ariel
These engaging retellings of familiar Bible stories are witty, often hilarious and always profound. They invite you to grapple with questions and issues that are often hidden in the original texts.
5½ x 8½, 192 pp, Quality PB, 978-1-59473-176-1 **$14.99**

Also available: **The Triumph of Eve Teacher's Guide**
8½ x 11, 44 pp, PB, 978-1-59473-152-5 **$8.99**

Wisdom in the Telling
Finding Inspiration and Grace in Traditional Folktales and Myths Retold
by Lorraine Hartin-Gelardi
6 x 9, 192 pp, HC, 978-1-59473-185-3 **$19.99**

Religious Etiquette / Reference

How to Be a Perfect Stranger, 4th Edition: The Essential Religious Etiquette Handbook
Edited by Stuart M. Matlins and Arthur J. Magida
The indispensable guidebook to help the well-meaning guest when visiting other people's religious ceremonies. A straightforward guide to the rituals and celebrations of the major religions and denominations in the United States and Canada from the perspective of an interested guest of any other faith, based on information obtained from authorities of each religion. Belongs in every living room, library and office. Covers:
African American Methodist Churches • Assemblies of God • Bahá'í • Baptist • Buddhist • Christian Church (Disciples of Christ) • Christian Science (Church of Christ, Scientist) • Churches of Christ • Episcopalian and Anglican • Hindu • Islam • Jehovah's Witnesses • Jewish • Lutheran • Mennonite/Amish • Methodist • Mormon (Church of Jesus Christ of Latter-day Saints) • Native American/First Nations • Orthodox Churches • Pentecostal Church of God • Presbyterian • Quaker (Religious Society of Friends) • Reformed Church in America/Canada • Roman Catholic • Seventh-day Adventist • Sikh • Unitarian Universalist • United Church of Canada • United Church of Christ

"The things Miss Manners forgot to tell us about religion." —*Los Angeles Times*

"Finally, for those inclined to undertake their own spiritual journeys ... tells visitors what to expect."
—*New York Times*

6 x 9, 432 pp, Quality PB, 978-1-59473-140-2 **$19.99**

The Perfect Stranger's Guide to Funerals and Grieving Practices: A Guide to Etiquette in Other People's Religious Ceremonies *Edited by Stuart M. Matlins*
6 x 9, 240 pp, Quality PB, 978-1-893361-20-1 **$16.95**

The Perfect Stranger's Guide to Wedding Ceremonies: A Guide to Etiquette in Other People's Religious Ceremonies *Edited by Stuart M. Matlins*
6 x 9, 208 pp, Quality PB, 978-1-893361-19-5 **$16.95**

Prayer / Meditation

Sacred Attention: A Spiritual Practice for Finding God in the Moment   *by Margaret D. McGee*
Framed on the Christian liturgical year, this inspiring guide explores ways to develop a practice of attention as a means of talking—and listening—to God.
6 x 9, 144 pp, Quality PB, 978-1-59473-291-1 **$16.99**

Women Pray: Voices through the Ages, from Many Faiths, Cultures and Traditions   *Edited and with Introductions by Monica Furlong*
5 x 7¼, 256 pp, Quality PB, 978-1-59473-071-9 **$15.99**

Women of Color Pray: Voices of Strength, Faith, Healing, Hope and Courage
Edited and with Introductions by Christal M. Jackson
Through these prayers, poetry, lyrics, meditations and affirmations, you will share in the strong and undeniable connection women of color share with God.
5 x 7¼, 208 pp, Quality PB, 978-1-59473-077-1 **$15.99**

Secrets of Prayer: A Multifaith Guide to Creating Personal Prayer in Your Life   *by Nancy Corcoran, CSJ*
This compelling, multifaith guidebook offers you companionship and encouragement on the journey to a healthy prayer life. 6 x 9, 160 pp, Quality PB, 978-1-59473-215-7 **$16.99**

Prayers to an Evolutionary God
by William Cleary; Afterword by Diarmuid O'Murchu
Inspired by the spiritual and scientific teachings of Diarmuid O'Murchu and Teilhard de Chardin, reveals that religion and science can be combined to create an expanding view of the universe—an evolutionary faith.
6 x 9, 208 pp, HC, 978-1-59473-006-1 **$21.99**

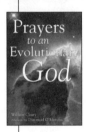

The Art of Public Prayer, 2nd Edition: Not for Clergy Only   *by Lawrence A. Hoffman, PhD*
6 x 9, 288 pp, Quality PB, 978-1-893361-06-5 **$19.99**

A Heart of Stillness: A Complete Guide to Learning the Art of Meditation   *by David A. Cooper*
5½ x 8½, 272 pp, Quality PB, 978-1-893361-03-4 **$18.99**

Meditation without Gurus: A Guide to the Heart of Practice   *by Clark Strand*
5½ x 8½, 192 pp, Quality PB, 978-1-893361-93-5 **$16.95**

Praying with Our Hands: 21 Practices of Embodied Prayer from the World's Spiritual Traditions
by Jon M. Sweeney; Photos by Jennifer J. Wilson; Foreword by Mother Tessa Bielecki; Afterword by Taitetsu Unno, PhD
8 x 8, 96 pp, 22 duotone photos, Quality PB, 978-1-893361-16-4 *$16.95*

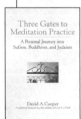

Three Gates to Meditation Practice: A Personal Journey into Sufism, Buddhism, and Judaism   *by David A. Cooper*
5½ x 8½, 240 pp, Quality PB, 978-1-893361-22-5 **$16.95**

Prayer / M. Basil Pennington, OCSO

Finding Grace at the Center, 3rd Edition: The Beginning of Centering Prayer
with Thomas Keating, OCSO, and Thomas E. Clarke, SJ; Foreword by Rev. Cynthia Bourgeault, PhD A practical guide to a simple and beautiful form of meditative prayer. 5 x 7¼, 128 pp, Quality PB, 978-1-59473-182-2 **$12.99**

The Monks of Mount Athos: A Western Monk's Extraordinary Spiritual Journey on Eastern Holy Ground
Foreword by Archimandrite Dionysios
Explores the landscape, monastic communities and food of Athos.
6 x 9, 352 pp, Quality PB, 978-1-893361-78-2 **$18.95**

Psalms: A Spiritual Commentary   *Illus. by Phillip Ratner*
Reflections on some of the most beloved passages from the Bible's most widely read book.
6 x 9, 176 pp, 24 full-page b/w illus., Quality PB, 978-1-59473-234-8 **$16.99**

The Song of Songs: A Spiritual Commentary   *Illus. by Phillip Ratner*
Explore the Bible's most challenging mystical text.
6 x 9, 160 pp, 14 full-page b/w illus., Quality PB, 978-1-59473-235-5 **$16.99**
HC, 978-1-59473-004-7 **$19.99**

Spirituality of the Seasons

Autumn: A Spiritual Biography of the Season
Edited by Gary Schmidt and Susan M. Felch; Illus. by Mary Azarian
Rejoice in autumn as a time of preparation and reflection. Includes Wendell Berry, David James Duncan, Robert Frost, A. Bartlett Giamatti, E. B. White, P. D. James, Julian of Norwich, Garret Keizer, Tracy Kidder, Anne Lamott, May Sarton.
6 x 9, 320 pp, b/w illus., Quality PB, 978-1-59473-118-1 **$18.99**

Spring: A Spiritual Biography of the Season
Edited by Gary Schmidt and Susan M. Felch; Illus. by Mary Azarian
Explore the gentle unfurling of spring and reflect on how nature celebrates rebirth and renewal. Includes Jane Kenyon, Lucy Larcom, Harry Thurston, Nathaniel Hawthorne, Noel Perrin, Annie Dillard, Martha Ballard, Barbara Kingsolver, Dorothy Wordsworth, Donald Hall, David Brill, Lionel Basney, Isak Dinesen, Paul Laurence Dunbar. 6 x 9, 352 pp, b/w illus., Quality PB, 978-1-59473-246-1 **$18.99**

Summer: A Spiritual Biography of the Season
Edited by Gary Schmidt and Susan M. Felch; Illus. by Barry Moser
"A sumptuous banquet…. These selections lift up an exquisite wholeness found within an everyday sophistication." — ★ *Publishers Weekly* starred review
Includes Anne Lamott, Luci Shaw, Ray Bradbury, Richard Selzer, Thomas Lynch, Walt Whitman, Carl Sandburg, Sherman Alexie, Madeleine L'Engle, Jamaica Kincaid.
6 x 9, 304 pp, b/w illus., Quality PB, 978-1-59473-183-9 **$18.99**; HC, 978-1-59473-083-2 **$21.99**

Winter: A Spiritual Biography of the Season
Edited by Gary Schmidt and Susan M. Felch; Illus. by Barry Moser
"This outstanding anthology features top-flight nature and spirituality writers on the fierce, inexorable season of winter…. Remarkably lively and warm, despite the icy subject." — ★ *Publishers Weekly* starred review
Includes Will Campbell, Rachel Carson, Annie Dillard, Donald Hall, Ron Hansen, Jane Kenyon, Jamaica Kincaid, Barry Lopez, Kathleen Norris, John Updike, E. B. White.
6 x 9, 288 pp, b/w illus., Deluxe PB w/ flaps, 978-1-893361-92-8 **$18.95**; HC, 978-1-893361-53-9 **$21.95**

Spirituality / Animal Companions

Blessing the Animals: Prayers and Ceremonies to Celebrate God's Creatures, Wild and Tame
Edited and with Introductions by Lynn L. Caruso
5¼ x 7¼, 256 pp, Quality PB, 978-1-59473-253-9 **$15.99**; HC, 978-1-59473-145-7 **$19.99**

Remembering My Pet: A Kid's Own Spiritual Workbook for When a Pet Dies
by Nechama Liss-Levinson, PhD, and Rev. Molly Phinney Baskette, MDiv; Foreword by Lynn L. Caruso
8 x 10, 48 pp, 2-color text, HC, 978-1-59473-221-8 **$16.99**

What Animals Can Teach Us about Spirituality: Inspiring Lessons from Wild and Tame Creatures
by Diana L. Guerrero
6 x 9, 176 pp, Quality PB, 978-1-893361-84-3 $16.95

Spirituality—A Week Inside

Lighting the Lamp of Wisdom: A Week Inside a Yoga Ashram   *by John Ittner; Foreword by Dr. David Frawley*
6 x 9, 192 pp, b/w photos, Quality PB, 978-1-893361-52-2 **$15.95**

Making a Heart for God: A Week Inside a Catholic Monastery   *by Dianne Aprile; Foreword by Brother Patrick Hart, OCSO*
6 x 9, 224 pp, b/w photos, Quality PB, 978-1-893361-49-2 **$16.95**

Waking Up: A Week Inside a Zen Monastery   *by Jack Maguire; Foreword by John Daido Loori, Roshi*
6 x 9, 224 pp, b/w photos, Quality PB, 978-1-893361-55-3 $16.95; HC, 978-1-893361-13-3 $21.95

Women's Interest

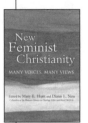

New Feminist Christianity: Many Voices, Many Views   *Edited by Mary E. Hunt and Diann L. Neu*
Insights from ministers and theologians, activists and leaders, artists and liturgists who are shaping the future.
Taken together, their voices offer a starting point for building new models of religious life and worship.
6 x 9, 384 pp, HC, 978-1-59473-285-0 **$24.99**

New Jewish Feminism: Probing the Past, Forging the Future
Edited by Rabbi Elyse Goldstein; Foreword by Anita Diamant
Looks at the growth and accomplishments of Jewish feminism and what they mean for Jewish women today
and tomorrow. Features the voices of women from every area of Jewish life, addressing the important issues
that concern Jewish women.
6 x 9, 480 pp, HC, 978-1-58023-359-0 **$24.99***

Dance—The Sacred Art: The Joy of Movement as a Spiritual Practice   *by Cynthia Winton-Henry*
5½ x 8½, 224 pp, Quality PB, 978-1-59473-268-3 **$16.99**

Daughters of the Desert: Stories of Remarkable Women from Christian, Jewish and Muslim Traditions
by Claire Rudolf Murphy, Meghan Nuttall Sayres, Mary Cronk Farrell, Sarah Conover and Betsy Wharton
5½ x 8½, 192 pp, Illus., Quality PB, 978-1-59473-106-8 **$14.99** Inc. reader's discussion guide
HC, 978-1-893361-72-0 **$19.95**

The Divine Feminine in Biblical Wisdom Literature: —Selections Annotated & Explained
Translation & Annotation by Rabbi Rami Shapiro; Foreword by Rev. Cynthia Bourgeault, PhD
5½ x 8½, 240 pp, Quality PB, 978-1-59473-109-9 **$16.99**

Divining the Body: Reclaim the Holiness of Your Physical Self   *by Jan Phillips*
8 x 8, 256 pp, Quality PB, 978-1-59473-080-1 **$16.99**

Honoring Motherhood: Prayers, Ceremonies & Blessings   *Edited and with Introductions by Lynn L. Caruso*
5 x 7¼, 272 pp, HC, 978-1-59473-239-3 **$19.99**

ReVisions: Seeing Torah through a Feminist Lens   *by Rabbi Elyse Goldstein*
5½ x 8½, 224 pp, Quality PB, 978-1-58023-117-6 **$16.95***

The Triumph of Eve & Other Subversive Bible Tales   *by Matt Biers-Ariel*
5½ x 8½, 192 pp, Quality PB, 978-1-59473-176-1 **$14.99**

Also available: **The Triumph of Eve Teacher's Guide**
8½ x 11, 44 pp, PB, 978-1-59473-152-5 **$8.99**

White Fire: A Portrait of Women Spiritual Leaders in America   *by Malka Drucker; Photos by Gay Block*
7 x 10, 320 pp, b/w photos, HC, 978-1-893361-64-5 **$24.95**

Woman Spirit Awakening in Nature: Growing Into the Fullness of Who You Are
by Nancy Barrett Chickerneo, PhD; Foreword by Eileen Fisher
8 x 8, 224 pp, b/w illus., Quality PB, 978-1-59473-250-8 **$16.99**

Women of Color Pray: Voices of Strength, Faith, Healing, Hope and Courage
Edited and with Introductions by Christal M. Jackson
5 x 7¼, 208 pp, Quality PB, 978-1-59473-077-1 **$15.99**

Women Pray: Voices through the Ages, from Many Faiths, Cultures and Traditions
Edited and with Introductions by Monica Furlong
5 x 7¼, 256 pp, Quality PB, 978-1-59473-071-9 **$15.99**

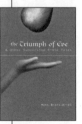

The Women's Haftarah Commentary: New Insights from Women Rabbis on the 54 Weekly Haftarah Portions,
the 5 Megillot & Special Shabbatot   *Edited by Rabbi Elyse Goldstein*
6 x 9, 560 pp, Quality PB, 978-1-58023-371-2 **$19.99***

The Women's Torah Commentary: New Insights from Women Rabbis on the 54 Weekly Torah Portions
Edited by Rabbi Elyse Goldstein
6 x 9, 496 pp, Quality PB, 978-1-58023-370-5 **$19.99**; HC, 978-1-58023-076-6 **$34.95***

* A book from Jewish Lights, SkyLight Paths' sister imprint

Spirituality

Creative Aging: Rethinking Retirement and Non-Retirement in a Changing World   *by Marjory Zoet Bankson*
Offers creative ways to nourish our calling and discover meaning and purpose in our older years.
6 x 9, 160 pp, Quality PB, 978-1-59473-281-2 **$16.99**

Laugh Your Way to Grace: Reclaiming the Spiritual Power of Humor
by Rev. Susan Sparks   A powerful, humorous case for laughter as a spiritual, healing path.
6 x 9, 176 pp, Quality PB, 978-1-59473-280-5 **$16.99**

Living into Hope: A Call to Spiritual Action for Such a Time as This
by Rev. Dr. Joan Brown Campbell; Foreword by Karen Armstrong
A visionary minister speaks out on the pressing issues that face us today, offering inspiration and challenge.
6 x 9, 144 pp (est), HC, 978-1-59473-283-6 **$21.99**

Claiming Earth as Common Ground: The Ecological Crisis through the Lens of Faith
by Andrea Cohen-Kiener; Foreword by Rev. Sally Bingham
Inspires us to work across denominational lines in order to fulfill our sacred imperative to care for God's
creation. 6 x 9, 192 pp, Quality PB, 978-1-59473-261-4 **$16.99**

Bread, Body, Spirit: Finding the Sacred in Food   *Edited and with Introductions by Alice Peck*
6 x 9, 224 pp, Quality PB, 978-1-59473-242-3 **$19.99**

Creating a Spiritual Retirement: A Guide to the Unseen Possibilities in Our Lives   *by Molly Srode*
6 x 9, 208 pp, b/w photos, Quality PB, 978-1-59473-050-4 **$14.99**

Finding Hope: Cultivating God's Gift of a Hopeful Spirit
by Marcia Ford; Foreword by Andrea Jaeger 8 x 8, 176 pp, Quality PB, 978-1-59473-211-9 **$16.99**

Hearing the Call across Traditions: Readings on Faith and Service
Edited by Adam Davis; Foreword by Eboo Patel 6 x 9, 352 pp, HC, 978-1-59473-264-5 **$29.99**

Honoring Motherhood: Prayers, Ceremonies & Blessings   *Edited and with Introductions by Lynn L. Caruso*
5 x 7¼, 272 pp, HC, 978-1-59473-239-3 **$19.99**

Journeys of Simplicity: Traveling Light with Thomas Merton, Bashō, Edward Abbey, Annie Dillard & Others   *by Philip Harnden*
5 x 7¼, 144 pp, Quality PB, 978-1-59473-181-5 **$12.99**; 128 pp, HC, 978-1-893361-76-8 **$16.95**

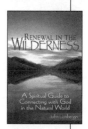

Keeping Spiritual Balance As We Grow Older: More than 65 Creative Ways to Use Purpose, Prayer, and the Power of Spirit to
Build a Meaningful Retirement   *by Molly and Bernie Srode* 8 x 8, 224 pp, Quality PB, 978-1-59473-042-9 **$16.99**

The Losses of Our Lives: The Sacred Gifts of Renewal in Everyday Loss   *by Dr. Nancy Copeland-Payton*
6 x 9, 192 pp, HC, 978-1-59473-271-3 **$19.99**

Money and the Way of Wisdom: Insights from the Book of Proverbs   *by Timothy J. Sandoval, PhD*
6 x 9, 192 pp, Quality PB, 978-1-59473-245-4 **$16.99**

Next to Godliness: Finding the Sacred in Housekeeping   *Edited by Alice Peck*   6 x 9, 224 pp, Quality PB, 978-1-59473-214-0 **$19.99**

Renewal in the Wilderness: A Spiritual Guide to Connecting with God in the Natural World   *by John Lionberger*
6 x 9, 176 pp, b/w photos, Quality PB, 978-1-59473-219-5 **$16.99**

Sacred Attention: A Spiritual Practice for Finding God in the Moment   *by Margaret D. McGee*
6 x 9, 144 pp, Quality PB, 978-1-59473-291-1 **$16.99**

Soul Fire: Accessing Your Creativity   *by Thomas Ryan, CSP*   6 x 9, 160 pp, Quality PB, 978-1-59473-243-0 **$16.99**

A Spirituality for Brokenness: Discovering Your Deepest Self in Difficult Times
by Terry Taylor   6 x 9, 176 pp, Quality PB, 978-1-59473-229-4 **$16.99**

Spiritually Incorrect: Finding God in All the *Wrong* Places   *by Dan Wakefield; Illus. by Marian DelVecchio*
5½ x 8½, 192 pp, b/w illus., Quality PB, 978-1-59473-137-2 **$15.99**

A Walk with Four Spiritual Guides: Krishna, Buddha, Jesus, and Ramakrishna
by Andrew Harvey 5½ x 8½, 192 pp, b/w photos & illus., Quality PB, 978-1-59473-138-9 **$15.99**

The Workplace and Spirituality: New Perspectives on Research and Practice
Edited by Dr. Joan Marques, Dr. Satinder Dhiman and Dr. Richard King
6 x 9, 256 pp, HC, 978-1-59473-260-7 **$29.99**

Spirituality & Crafts

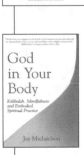

Beading—The Creative Spirit: Finding Your Sacred Center through the Art of Beadwork *by Rev. Wendy Ellsworth*
Invites you on a spiritual pilgrimage into the kaleidoscope world of glass and color.
7 x 9, 240 pp, 8-page color insert, 40+ b/w photos and 40 diagrams, Quality PB, 978-1-59473-267-6 $18.99

Contemplative Crochet: A Hands-On Guide for Interlocking Faith and Craft
by Cindy Crandall-Frazier; Foreword by Linda Skolnik
Illuminates the spiritual lessons you can learn through crocheting.
7 x 9, 208 pp, b/w photos, Quality PB, 978-1-59473-238-6 **$16.99**

The Knitting Way: A Guide to Spiritual Self-Discovery
by Linda Skolnik and Janice MacDaniels
Examines how you can explore and strengthen your spiritual life through knitting.
7 x 9, 240 pp, b/w photos, Quality PB, 978-1-59473-079-5 **$16.99**

The Painting Path: Embodying Spiritual Discovery through Yoga, Brush and Color
by Linda Novick; Foreword by Richard Segalman
Explores the divine connection you can experience through art.
7 x 9, 208 pp, 8-page color insert, plus b/w photos, Quality PB, 978-1-59473-226-3 **$18.99**

The Quilting Path: A Guide to Spiritual Discovery through Fabric, Thread and Kabbalah *by Louise Silk*
Explores how to cultivate personal growth through quilt making.
7 x 9, 192 pp, b/w photos and illus., Quality PB, 978-1-59473-206-5 **$16.99**

The Scrapbooking Journey: A Hands-On Guide to Spiritual Discovery
by Cory Richardson-Lauve; Foreword by Stacy Julian
Reveals how this craft can become a practice used to deepen and shape your life.
7 x 9, 176 pp, 8-page color insert, plus b/w photos, Quality PB, 978-1-59473-216-4 **$18.99**

The Soulwork of Clay: A Hands-On Approach to Spirituality
by Marjory Zoet Bankson; Photos by Peter Bankson
Takes you through the seven-step process of making clay into a pot, drawing parallels at each stage to the process of spiritual growth. 7 x 9, 192 pp, b/w photos, Quality PB, 978-1-59473-249-2 **$16.99**

Kabbalah / Enneagram
(Books from Jewish Lights Publishing, SkyLight Paths' sister imprint)

Cast in God's Image: Discover Your Personality Type Using the Enneagram and Kabbalah
by Rabbi Howard A. Addison 7 x 9, 176 pp, Quality PB, 978-1-58023-124-4 **$16.95**

Ehyeh: A Kabbalah for Tomorrow *by Dr. Arthur Green* 6 x 9, 224 pp, Quality PB, 978-1-58023-213-5 **$16.99**

The Enneagram and Kabbalah, 2nd Edition: Reading Your Soul *by Rabbi Howard A. Addison*
6 x 9, 192 pp, Quality PB, 978-1-58023-229-6 **$16.99**

The Gift of Kabbalah: Discovering the Secrets of Heaven, Renewing Your Life on Earth *by Tamar Frankiel, PhD*
6 x 9, 256 pp, Quality PB, 978-1-58023-141-1 **$16.95**

God in Your Body: Kabbalah, Mindfulness and Embodied Spiritual Practice *by Jay Michaelson*
6 x 9, 272 pp, Quality PB, 978-1-58023-304-0 **$18.99**

Kabbalah: A Brief Introduction for Christians *by Tamar Frankiel, PhD*
5½ x 8½, 208 pp, Quality PB, 978-1-58023-303-3 **$16.99**

Zohar: Annotated & Explained *Translation & Annotation by Daniel C. Matt; Foreword by Andrew Harvey*
5½ x 8½, 176 pp, Quality PB, 978-1-893361-51-5 **$15.99**

Spiritual Practice

Laugh Your Way to Grace: Reclaiming the Spiritual Power of Humor
by Rev. Susan Sparks A powerful, humorous case for laughter as a spiritual, healing path.
6 x 9, 176 pp, Quality PB, 978-1-59473-280-5 $16.99

Haiku—The Sacred Art: A Spiritual Practice in Three Lines
by Margaret D. McGee Introduces haiku as a simple and effective way of tapping into the sacred moments that permeate everyday living. 5½ x 8½, 192 pp, Quality PB, 978-1-59473-269-0 **$16.99**

Dance—The Sacred Art: The Joy of Movement as a Spiritual Practice
by Cynthia Winton-Henry Invites all of us, regardless of experience, into the possibility of dance/movement as a spiritual practice. 5½ x 8½, 224 pp, Quality PB, 978-1-59473-268-3 **$16.99**

Spiritual Adventures in the Snow: Skiing & Snowboarding as Renewal for Your Soul
by Dr. Marcia McFee and Rev. Karen Foster; Foreword by Paul Arthur
Explores snow sports as tangible experiences of the spiritual essence of our bodies and the earth.
5½ x 8½, 208 pp, Quality PB, 978-1-59473-270-6 **$16.99**

Divining the Body: Reclaim the Holiness of Your Physical Self *by Jan Phillips* 8 x 8, 256 pp, Quality PB, 978-1-59473-080-1 **$16.99**

Everyday Herbs in Spiritual Life: A Guide to Many Practices
by Michael J. Caduto; Foreword by Rosemary Gladstar 7 x 9, 208 pp, 20+ b/w illus., Quality PB, 978-1-59473-174-7 **$16.99**

The Gospel of Thomas: A Guidebook for Spiritual Practice *by Ron Miller; Translations by Stevan Davies*
6 x 9, 160 pp, Quality PB, 978-1-59473-047-4 **$14.99**

Hospitality—The Sacred Art: Discovering the Hidden Spiritual Power of Invitation and Welcome
by Rev. Nanette Sawyer; Foreword by Rev. Dirk Ficca 5½ x 8½, 208 pp, Quality PB, 978-1-59473-228-7 **$16.99**

Labyrinths from the Outside In: Walking to Spiritual Insight—A Beginner's Guide
by Donna Schaper and Carole Ann Camp 6 x 9, 208 pp, b/w illus. and photos, Quality PB, 978-1-893361-18-8 **$16.95**

Practicing the Sacred Art of Listening: A Guide to Enrich Your Relationships and Kindle Your Spiritual Life
by Kay Lindahl 8 x 8, 176 pp, Quality PB, 978-1-893361-85-0 **$16.95**

Recovery—The Sacred Art: The Twelve Steps as Spiritual Practice *by Rami Shapiro; Foreword by Joan Borysenko, PhD*
5½ x 8½, 240 pp, Quality PB, 978-1-59473-259-1 **$16.99**

Running—The Sacred Art: Preparing to Practice *by Dr. Warren A. Kay; Foreword by Kristin Armstrong*
5½ x 8½, 160 pp, Quality PB, 978-1-59473-227-0 **$16.99**

The Sacred Art of Bowing: Preparing to Practice *by Andi Young*
5½ x 8½, 128 pp, b/w illus., Quality PB, 978-1-893361-82-9 **$14.95**

The Sacred Art of Chant: Preparing to Practice *by Ana Hernández*
5½ x 8½, 192 pp, Quality PB, 978-1-59473-036-8 **$15.99**

The Sacred Art of Fasting: Preparing to Practice *by Thomas Ryan, CSP*
5½ x 8½, 192 pp,, Quality PB, 978-1-59473-078-8 **$15.99**

The Sacred Art of Forgiveness: Forgiving Ourselves and Others through God's Grace *by Marcia Ford*
8 x 8, 176 pp, Quality PB, 978-1-59473-175-4 **$18.99**

The Sacred Art of Listening: Forty Reflections for Cultivating a Spiritual Practice *by Kay Lindahl; Illus. by Amy Schnapper*
8 x 8, 160 pp, b/w illus., Quality PB, 978-1-893361-44-7 **$16.99**

The Sacred Art of Lovingkindness: Preparing to Practice *by Rabbi Rami Shapiro; Foreword by Marcia Ford*
5½ x 8½, 176 pp Quality PB, 978-1-59473-151-8 **$16.99**

Sacred Attention: A Spiritual Practice for Finding God in the Moment *by Margaret D. McGee*
6 x 9, 144 pp Quality PB, 978-1-59473-291-1 **$16.99**

Sacred Speech: A Practical Guide for Keeping Spirit in Your Speech *by Rev. Donna Schaper*
6 x 9, 176 pp, Quality PB, 978-1-59473-068-9 **$15.99** HC, 978-1-893361-74-4 **$21.95**

Soul Fire: Accessing Your Creativity *by Thomas Ryan, CSP* 6 x 9, 160 pp, Quality PB, 978-1-59473-243-0 **$16.99**

Thanking & Blessing—The Sacred Art: Spiritual Vitality through Gratefulness
by Jay Marshall, PhD; Foreword by Philip Gulley 5½ x 8½, 176 pp, Quality PB, 978-1-59473-231-7 **$16.99**

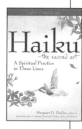

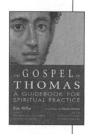
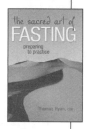

About SKYLIGHT PATHS Publishing

SkyLight Paths Publishing is creating a place where people of different spiritual traditions come together for challenge and inspiration, a place where we can help each other understand the mystery that lies at the heart of our existence.

Through spirituality, our religious beliefs are increasingly becoming a part of our lives—rather than *apart* from our lives. While many of us may be more interested than ever in spiritual growth, we may be less firmly planted in traditional religion. Yet, we do want to deepen our relationship to the sacred, to learn from our own as well as from other faith traditions, and to practice in new ways.

SkyLight Paths sees both believers and seekers as a community that increasingly transcends traditional boundaries of religion and denomination—people wanting to learn from each other, *walking together, finding the way.*

For your information and convenience, at the back of this book we have provided a list of other SkyLight Paths books you might find interesting and useful. They cover the following subjects:

Buddhism / Zen	Global Spiritual	Monasticism
Catholicism	Perspectives	Mysticism
Children's Books	Gnosticism	Poetry
Christianity	Hinduism /	Prayer
Comparative	Vedanta	Religious Etiquette
Religion	Inspiration	Retirement
Current Events	Islam / Sufism	Spiritual Biography
Earth-Based	Judaism	Spiritual Direction
Spirituality	Kabbalah	Spirituality
Enneagram	Meditation	Women's Interest
	Midrash Fiction	Worship

Or phone, fax, mail or e-mail to: **SKYLIGHT PATHS** Publishing
Sunset Farm Offices, Route 4 • P.O. Box 237 • Woodstock, Vermont 05091
Tel: (802) 457-4000 • Fax: (802) 457-4004 • www.skylightpaths.com
Credit card orders: (800) 962-4544 (8:30AM–5:30PM ET Monday–Friday)
Generous discounts on quantity orders. SATISFACTION GUARANTEED. Prices subject to change.